The Karimjee Jivanjee Family

Merchant Princes of East Africa 1800 - 2000

The Karimjee Jivanjee Family
Merchant Princes
of East Africa 1800 - 2000

Gijsbert Oonk
Erasmus University Rotterdam
The Netherlands

Foreword by Hatim A. Karimjee

PALLAS PUBLICATIONS

Publisher	Pallas Publications · Amsterdam University Press, Amsterdam 2009
Cover & Layout Design	NL ontwerp, Nandan Lemmers, Warnsveld, The Netherlands
Lithography	Marc Gijzen, Leidschendam, The Netherlands
ISBN	978 90 8555 027 3
e-ISBN	978 90 4851 172 3
NUR	640

© Gijsbert Oonk / Pallas Publications · Amsterdam University Press, Amsterdam 2009

All rights reserved. Without limiting the rights under copyright reserved above, no part of this book may be reproduced, stored in or introduced into a retrieval system, or transmitted, in any form or by any means (electronic, mechanical, photocopying, recording or otherwise) without the written permission of both the copyright owner and the author of the book.

Yusufali Karimjee, 1882 - 1966.

Abdulla Mohamedali Karimjee, 1899 - 1978.

Abdulkarim Yusufali Karimjee, 1906 - 1977, (second from left).

Tayabali Karimjee, 1897 - 1987.

Table of Contents

	Foreword by Hatim Karimjee	10
1	Introduction	13
2	Connecting Asia and Africa	21
3	The Making of a Trading Empire, 1880 - 1924	33
	PORTRAIT Yusufali Karimjee, 1882 - 1966	48
4	From Trades to Estates, 1925 - 1963	58
	A SHORT HISTORY OF SISAL	67
	PORTRAIT Abdulla Mohamedali Karimjee, 1899 - 1978	90
5	Political Turmoil and Economic Decline, 1964 - 1990	104
	PORTRAIT Abdulkarim Yusufali Karimjee, 1906 - 1977	110
6	Religion, Politics and Charity, 1880 - 2000	127
	PORTRAIT Tayabali Karimjee, 1897 - 1987	138
7	Explaining the Past While Looking at the Future	148
	Acknowledgement and sources	157
	List of Nationalised Properties	161
	Notes	169

African workers at a Karimjee sisal estate in the 1950s.

List of maps and tables

Map 1	Monsoon winds in the Indian Ocean	22
Map 2	Ethnic distribution of Asian communities in Stonetown, Zanzibar	23
Map 3	Political map of East Africa	58
Table 1	Distribution of directorships in Karimjee Jivanjee & Co., 1950	65
Table 2	Sisal production of Tanganyika by proprietors in 1954	68
Table 3	A new generation of Karimjee managers	108
Table 4	Major shareholder meeting 1987	120
Table 5	Asian sub-groupings in East Africa by religion, language and caste	128
Table 6	List of charities and their values	133

Foreword

There are many reasons for undertaking this mission to write the history of our family. It is a fascinating adventure spanning 200 years of survival, struggle, historical sentiments and achievements. More importantly, however, it is a tribute to our ancestors who crossed the kalapani (black waters) in a dhow from India to Africa at the beginning of the 19th century. Our family owes so much to those who had the courage to travel across an unknown ocean to an unknown and forbidding continent. Having reached Zanzibar, our ancestors prospered in the face of amazing difficulties through determination, hard work and an enterprising spirit.

I am honoured to dedicate this history of the Karimjee Jivanjee Family to our ancestors.

This history has also been written for the benefit of the present generation, many of whom have heard only bits and pieces of family history but have never seen the broader picture. For some of them Africa and India have become a far away holiday destination, whereas for our family these continents represent our roots. This book seeks to remind them of the past achievements of our forefathers and our family business.

Perhaps the most important goal of this history project is to tell future generations of family members the story of our historic journey from India to Africa: how we faced challenges, experienced tragedies, became wealthy, and why after so many years we are respected and held in high esteem by political, business and community leaders. I have always feared that the story of our family's history would eventually be forgotten especially to our new generations who have migrated to and settled in many countries all over the globe.

The family is still united after more than nine generations spanning over more than two hundred years and its businesses still remain in the family's hands and under family management. These are astonishing feats in themselves. I would like to think that there are many lessons to be learned from our unique experiences that would benefit today's business community as well as future entrepreneurs.

I have been so keen to see this history written that I have talked about it many, many times. The project had some false starts but the idea never left my mind. My greatest concern was that our repository of memories of past events was gradually slipping away as our family elders passed away. Many were the times that I asked my father to record his memories of our family business and after his retirement I asked him to write his story. For various reasons he never got round to this but he did spend many evenings recounting happy times and sad days as did many of our forefathers to their siblings.

I met Gijsbert Oonk when he came to my office to collect material for his book *Asians in East Africa. Images, histories and portraits* (Arkel 2004). The excellent quality of that publication gave me confidence to ask him if he would be interested in writing our family's history. He readily agreed and so began the tale of this great adventure spanning nearly 200 years of our presence in East Africa today.

It is strange how stories handed down to me by my parents differ from stories handed down by other family elders to their children. Like all oral history accuracy fades away with time and interpretations and wishful thinking takes its place. It has been a tremendous challenge for Gijsbert to make sense out of the different variations on the same tale and I admire his tenacity and patience in seeking the truth as far as it was possible after so long. As a complete stranger to the family he had difficulties with names, as there are so many different ways of pronouncing and spelling a name. Nevertheless Gijsbert is above all an academic and a historian and his approach was always to cross reference and look for other sources to reach the truth. On many occasions I challenged him on his interpretation but he proved me wrong with hard facts. If only my father and many of my aunts and uncles were alive today it would have been so much easier to reach a clearer understanding of our history.

In the final analysis, this is Gijsbert Oonk's story of the Karimjee Jivanjee family; it is the author's version of the family, arrived at through his research. He conducted interviews with family members, people from our community, but also outsiders, staff and employees. In addition he studied our business documents going back more than a century. He went to the archives and scanned complete photo albums of our parents and grandparents. His story presents the 'grand picture' of our family with detailed insights and anecdotes.

It was necessary to establish cut off points for the history as well as for the family tree. It isn't history if it is happening in the present and a family tree never stops growing as new births, marriages and deaths occur. Studying our post-2004 history may well be a project for the future. After all, it took us 200 years to write this one!

The family are very grateful to Gijsbert for the successful completion of this history. He took time off from his teaching and research assignments at Erasmus University Rotterdam. It took much longer than he anticipated, because it had to be rewritten as better sources became available. Writing this story was long overdue and some may say that we got round to it too late. But I am glad that this life mission has finally been achieved.

Hatim A. Karimjee
Dar es Salaam, 21 May 2009

Karimjee Jivanjee Darema tea factory in the 1950s. The transition from trades to estates is described in chapter four.

CHAPTER 1

Introduction

This book is an account of the business history of the Karimjee Jivanjee family from Tanzania. Much more than a 'rags to riches' story, it is also a story of 'social responsibility', and political ambitions. It is a story of trading with Europe, Africa and East Asia in the late 19th century and making money in the sisal industry just after the Second World War. It is a story of adventures, of winning and losing, and of travelling around the globe in sailing ships and steamers. The Karimjees started trading from Zanzibar with India, Ceylon, Kenya, Mauritius, Japan and China, as well as the UK, Germany and other European countries. They were once one of the largest landowners in Tanzania, producing tea, coffee, sisal, cashew nuts and other agricultural products. Today, the Karimjees are the authorised distributors of Toyota cars in Tanzania. In short, therefore, this book describes 200 years of a remarkable business history, where business, politics, social welfare and family walked hand in hand.

The Karimjees originally came from Mandvi, which is a small seaport in Kutch in north-west India. They are Muslims - more specifically Bohras. They were originally petty traders who probably had a background in agriculture. During the famines and economic hardship of the early 19th century, they were forced to look for new ways of making a living. One option was to sail to Zanzibar. The founding father of the Karimjee Jivanjee family, Jivanjee Buddhabhoy, arrived in Zanzibar in 1818. There he became part of a South Asian community on the island that probably consisted of fewer than 1000 people, most of whom were young men.

The history of business in East Africa is the history of exceptional African, Arab, European and Indian families. Nevertheless, most of these family businesses would only survive one or two generations. Jivanjee started his modest trading business just before the important local South Asian kings of trade and commerce such as Tharia Thopan (1823 - 1891), Sewa Haji (1851 - 1897), Allidina Visram (1851 - 1916) and Nasser Veerjee (1865 - 1942). These merchant princes were among the principal financiers of East African caravan trades in the 19th century. However, they have now vanished from the economic playing fields of East Africa, whereas the firm of Karimjee Jivanjee & Co. is still active in Dar es Salaam. In the 1950s, they were referred to as 'The Merchant Princes of East Africa'.[1] Having first arrived in East Africa almost 200 years ago, the Karimjees preceded the current major South Asian business tycoons in East Africa, such as the Mehtas, the Madhvanis and the Chandarias.

In those two centuries the Karimjees have had to navigate through rapidly shifting political and economic environments. In 1832, Sultan Seyyid Said from Oman transferred his capital to Zanzibar. The Arabs spread their political and economic influence to Zanzibar and Pemba as well as key locations on the East African coast such as Bagamoyo, Mombasa, Malindi and Kilwa. The British and the Germans, realising the extent of the Sultan's influence, decided to assign him a special status in his territories at the Berlin Conference of 1884. Eventually, the partition of Africa offered the Sultan a claim to the islands of Zanzibar and Pemba as well as to a coastal strip of land. The abolition of the slave trade weakened the Sultan's empire and, bit-by-bit, he lost more land to the new European colonisers. Finally, the British and Germans came to a (political) agreement with the Sultan to sell his possessions on the mainland. By the end of the 19th century, very little land remained under the Sultan's control. The British and Germans were now the rulers of Zanzibar and East Africa.

The complex political economy of Zanzibar in the 19th century is often described as a triangular relationship between Arab and European rulers and businessmen at the top, South Asians in the middle, and Swahilis at the bottom of the social ladder. At the top were the Western firms, who were rational, well funded, and often based on the joint stock principle. The Arabs owned plantations and produced cloves and spices. Some were involved in the caravan trade, collecting ivory from the mainland, and in the slave trade. The Indian moneylenders, who neither owned land nor ventured into the interior themselves, were half way up the social ladder. They often financed the activities of the Arabs. In addition, the South Asian family firms acted as intermediaries between European firms and Arabs, or between Swahili producers and European traders. The Swahilis were often described as 'ignorant', 'living day by day' and ultimately being incapable of rational economic behaviour in terms of investments and reinvestments in profitable businesses. The reality, however, was more complex than this simple social model, especially as regards the South Asians, who could be found at both the top and bottom ends of society.[2]

The Karimjees have seen both sides of society. They accumulated capital and a good name between 1824 and 1861. Nevertheless, one of the descendants of Buddhaboy, Karimjee Jivanjee, lost all of his investments in the 1860s. He kept his good name, however, and he was able to re-establish Karimjee Jivanjee & Co within a decade. This experience probably did a great deal to build the strength of the future generations of Karimjees.

For various reasons, many of the early South Asian kings of trade lost their prominence in the late 19th and early 20th centuries. Some failed to cope with the changing political and economic factors. Others failed to find suitable successors within their families. The Karimjee Jivanjee family is one of the notable exceptions. They arrived as traders, divided the business among the brothers, and almost went bankrupt, before reviving their business to eventually become one of the most important South Asian business families in East Africa prior to the Second World War. They would later lose a significant share of their properties, businesses and influence in Tanzania following the Arusha Declaration and nationalisation of businesses and properties in 1967 and 1971. But once more they survived a complex political and economic change after Tanzania became independent, and now they have revived their fortunes again and their business is flourishing.

This background alone would have been sufficient reason to study the processes and stages of evolution of the business power of the Karimjee Jivanjee family. But there are even more important reasons for attempting this work because academic research into African history mostly focuses on political developments and an analysis of socio-economic changes. On the surface, Asian families play no role in these accounts. The family history described in this work, however, shows that Asian families played a vital economic and political role in East Africa. They contributed to the economic development of the country and the welfare of the workers, and they played an important role in the independence movement.

Meaningful in-depth studies 'from within' are hard to find in business history. This study mainly relies on sources from within the family, whereas the bulk of economic and business history is based on colonial sources. Business records, family correspondence and photographs were made available. In addition, numerous interviews were conducted with family members and outsiders. Together, they show a varied, dynamic and changing picture of a family, its businesses, and East Africa

THE BUSINESS ORGANISATION AS SEEN THROUGH ITS LETTERHEADS

The original name of the parent company was Karimjee Jivanjee & Co. Ltd. This firm was established in 1825 in Zanzibar and moved its headquarters to Dar es Salaam in 1943. However, in the 1920s and 1930s, the letterheads show the rapid expansion of the Karimjee Jivanjee business. This expansion resulted in new Karimjee Jivanjee companies, such as Karimjee Jivanjee Estates Ltd., and Karimjee Properties Ltd. The formal separation of the trading activities, the real estate and the agricultural production was necessary in order to clarify and control profit margins, expenses and legal solutions. In general, the parent company remained Karimjee Jivanjee & Co. Ltd. Each company was headed by its own managing director and managed by its Board of Directors, which consisted of family members.

Letterheads of the major Karimjee Companies in the 1920s-1950s.
The letterheads also mention the names of the directors.

as a whole, all from the perspective of the family. At the same time, the major events of East African political and economic history are used as the mirror reflecting this family history.

The history of a business empire is essentially a series of entrepreneurial decisions. The importance of innovative entrepreneurship is rightly emphasised by Joseph Schumpeter. However, 'innovation' is not self-evident. It acquires meaning in a specific economic environment. Therefore it is important to describe the context of African society and its history. In addition, it is important to see entrepreneurial decisions in the context of the family's history. The great advantage of this research is that we were able to balance the 'economic environment' and the 'context of the Karimjee family history' in order to clarify the paths and directions taken by the family.

This balance is by no means static or easy. In fact, the local, national and international economy is constantly changing and may create new opportunities and challenges, as well as the experience of exploiting new opportunities. From a family point of view, decisions have to be made about marriages, and the management of the business, and the allocation of management resources. Who is willing to work abroad? In times of economic prosperity and political stability, the balance between economic factors and the family's choices may appear pretty straightforward. However, in times of economic decline, losses and depression as well as in times of political instability, choices have major consequences for the future welfare of the family. This Karimjee Jivanjee family history is an attempt to show how this balance emerged and developed over a long period of time. In other words, this is the 200-year business history of the Karimjee Jivanjee family.

This book is divided into seven chapters. There are two basic organising principles. First and foremost, the history of the Karimjee Jivanjee family is presented in chronological order. The story starts when the first Karimjee arrived in Zanzibar in the 1820s and it ends with the current situation. The important transitions and periods when the family and its businesses had to adapt to East Africa are highlighted throughout the chapters. Following this introductory chapter, the cultural and economic connections between Asia and Africa are emphasised: how and why did the Karimjee family shift their business from South Asia to East Africa? The third chapter highlights the early development of the Karimjee trading business and describes how they developed from petty traders to the most important trading partner in East Africa for European, American and Asian firms and families (1880 - 1924). Chapter four highlights the importance of the transition from 'trades to estates' as the Karimjees decided to diversify in coffee, tea and sisal plantations. This was an entirely new venture for the family. How and why did they become the biggest Asian sisal barons in East Africa between 1925 and 1963? Chapter five covers a period of political turmoil and economic decline after Tanzania gained its independence (1964 - 1990). This was a dark chapter for many Asians in East Africa. The Asian Expulsion between 1968 and 1972 was one of the most traumatic experiences in the history of Asian Africans. The sixth chapter emphasises the importance for East Africa of the social and political contributions made by the Karimjee Jivanjee family between 1880 and 2000. This chapter shows how the business family got involved in the larger society of East Africa and played an important role in the emancipation of East African Asians. The family were also active in the Tanzanian independence movement, in addition to working through various charitable institutions to provide educational scholarships and finance schools, hospitals, mosques and community and social welfare facilities, including the well

A letter of registration of Esmailjee Jivanjee, dated 8 March 1895. Esmailjee separated from his brother Karimjee in 1861, see chapter two.

اقر مسعود وعمران ابنا سعيد خادن السليمانيان ان عليها
واسماعيل جيوجي البقمي نصف قرش وسبعه وثلاثين قرشا ماينبي
قرشا والفقري صرف البلد معجلان عليها الى المدة انقضا وعشرة
اشهر زمانا هذا اليوم وقدارهنا معه هذا ثبتها التي لها باض
الجزيرة الخضرا المسما زوان المحا وغلشا بنب سعيد سليمان قبله
وبنت سعيد خمّاس مخيا واوزاد عبدالرحمن صلح كوسا وعبدالله سعد
مطلعها وحدعدها وجميع ما اشتمل عليها من اشجار الفر نفار التاحيل
والامبا وغير ذكر من جميع الاشجار هنا مقبوض انها فيها تصرف
مادام هذه الحق عليها باقيا اقرار منها به ذلك بتاريخ يوم ٢٥
شهر شعبان ١٣١٢ وكتبه الفقير سد حامد خلفان عبيد خادم بني شكينله

Registration No. 216 of 1895 (Class B)

Produced by Esmailji Jivunji and registered at his request at the Regn. Office of the Z'bar Govt. dated this 8th day of March 95.

First Minister of the Z'bar Govt.

Cursetji Cawasji
Registrar

known Karimjee Hall. The seventh and last chapter focuses on the Karimjee family in the 21st century, whilst also reflecting on the major causes of the success, persistence and instinct for survival that the family has consistently demonstrated for the last two centuries.

The biographies of the four historical champions of the Karimjee Jivanjee family form the second organising principle of this work. Without denying the importance of other individuals in the family, and the importance of the extended family as a whole, these four persons merited a separate introduction. Two of them were knighted for their contributions to East African society as a whole, namely Yusufali Karimjee (1882 - 1966) and Tayabali Karimjee (1897 - 1987). Yusufali was an extremely innovative trader who explored markets from Japan to Hannover. At the same time he supported the modern factions of the Bohra community. He gave generous donations to numerous schools, mosques and community halls. His short biography appears in chapter three, in relation to the expansion of the trading business. The biography of Tayabali Karimjee is in chapter six, where his charitable and political contributions are highlighted. He wrote himself into Zanzibar history as member of the Legislative Council by walking out after the Council passed the Clove Monopoly Bill on 23rd July 1937. On that day, all the Indian shops in Zanzibar closed their shops.

The third historical champion was Abdulla Karimjee (1899 - 1978). His portrait can be found in chapter four. His major economic contribution relates to the growth of the tea, coffee and sisal plantations. He became the sisal baron of the Karimjee family. However, he was also a very social and charismatic figure, with quite a presence in international elite circles: he was invited to the Coronation of Queen Elizabeth the Second and he was made an OBE (Officer of the British Empire). The fourth historical champion was Abdulkarim Karimjee (1906 - 1977). He combined the heroic features of all of the Karimjees in one person. He was a shrewd and entrepreneurial businessman, a fine politician and a great supporter of charities. He was made a CBE (Commander of the British Empire). His biography would fit in all the chapters of this study. Nevertheless, since he remained as one of the few Karimjees in East Africa after the Nationalisation of Properties in 1971, it seemed appropriate to incorporate his biography in chapter five, which covers a period of political turmoil and economic decline.

In short, the Karimjees have set a standard for doing business in an international and complex environment. They all played their role in loosening racial and sectarian boundaries. They served the colonial officials as well as the Tanzanian independence movement and in the end, from humble beginnings in the small seaport of Mandvi in Gujarat in India, they ultimately became 'world citizens' before the term was even invented.

CHAPTER 1 · INTRODUCTION

Gujarati craftsmen still build wooden 'dhows' in the Mandvi harbour that are designed for crossing the Indian Ocean from India to East Africa. Pictures by author, January 2007.

CHAPTER 2

Connecting Asia and Africa

The founding father of the Karimjee Jivanjee family was Buddhaboy Noormuhammed. He was a Bohra (Muslim) trader in the seaport of Mandvi in Western India in the early 19th century. There, he owned a small hardware business. In those days the economic prospects were predominantly dependent on the agricultural produce in the region. At the same time, however, Gujarat was opening up to a wider world. In the early 19th century, Mandvi was connected with South Indian ports in Gujarat and Maharasthra, like Porbander, Surat and Bombay. More importantly, it was also linked to Arab ports like Aden and Muscat and the trading centres of Mogadishu, Zanzibar and Malindi along the north-eastern coast of Africa. The sailors of Mandvi were known to be adventurous and it is said that Vasco da Gama made use of a sailor from Mandvi (Ahmed ibn Majid) to navigate from Zanzibar to India. This is but a small indication of the importance of South Asian and Arab traders in the Indian Ocean region.

Mandvi still produces hand-built dhows and small boats. The craftsmanship of the South Asian shipbuilders is still alive and well and can be observed in the harbour of Mandvi. Currently, more than ten smaller dhows and six or seven bigger ones are being built at any one time. This is a clear reminder of its long seafaring history. Most ships are built by hand and only a few nails are used. The models and the designs used are a clear mirror of the past. This is one of the amazing features of Mandvi. It is easy to see how the constant and ongoing construction of dhows continually reminded the businessmen in Mandvi that there was a bigger world to be discovered elsewhere. In this chapter we will outline this process of linking Africa and Asia as it applies to the Karimjee Jivanjee family.

One day, on a visit to Mandvi, the chief Custom Master of the Sultan of Oman in Zanzibar, the Indian Jairam Sewji, approached Buddhaboy. He used to travel from Zanzibar to Aden and West India every two or three years. Sewji was a very rich and influential figure in the Indian Ocean region. He obviously talked to Buddhaboy about the economic potential of East Africa and the business opportunities in Zanzibar. As a result, Buddhaboy decided to send his son, Jivanjee, to Zanzibar to explore the economic options for his family.

Family records reveal that Jivanjee opened his own hardware shop in Zanzibar in 1818. In 1825 he established his own trading company, Jivanjee Buddhaboy & Co, which exported cloves and copra to India and imported German and American cloth (Americani). This company was just one of the many Indian firms established around that time by various zealous businessmen from India. However, only a few businesses 'survived' for more than 10 years. Jivanjee not only 'survived', he established the name 'Jivanjee' in Zanzibar, a name that is still well-known in East Africa today.[3]

If we study the map of the Indian Ocean, it is not surprising to find that there is a long history involving the exchange of trades, ideas, crafts and people between West India, the Arab countries and East Africa. The rhythm of the monsoons placed a constraint on direct trade between the continents. From November to March, the familiar magnificent dhows sailed from West India to East Africa, making the return journey from April to October. The trade in cotton cloth, ivory, and spices was profitable, but fraught with risk. Many traders did not return home safely. Rough seas, pirates, and various diseases claimed the lives of many traders and early adventurers.

MAP 1 MONSOON WINDS IN THE INDIAN OCEAN

These early contacts between Indians and East Africans go back at least 2000 years. The first undisputed written evidence of these early contacts is the Periplus of the Erythraean Sea written by a Greek trade merchant in the first century A.D. The earliest sizeable trading posts emerged along the East African coast in the early centuries A.D. When Vasco da Gama arrived in Mozambique, Mombasa, and Lindi in 1497, he was surprised at the number of Arabs and Indians he encountered there.[4] Nevertheless, it was only in the 19th century that South Asians started to settle in East Africa, and the Bohra Jivanjee Buddhaboy was one of these settlers.

In the early 19th century, very few Bohras were to be found in Zanzibar. In 1872 the famous British explorer Richard F. Burton wrote of the Indian Muslims in Zanzibar: "The Indian Muslims on the island and the coast were numbered in 1844 at 600-700. Besides a few Bohras and Memons, Zanzibar contains about 100 Khojas."[5] In other words, the Jivanjee family was part of a very small Bohra community in Zanzibar. They lived in a few streets in a small neighbourhood in what is now known as Stone Town in Zanzibar. Before they built their first mosque, they probably held their prayer services in one of these houses. The Bhoras were, and still are, known as an extremely close-knit, self-contained community in all areas, not only in those concerned with religion. They – like other migrant communities – tended to live in the same streets and areas in the cities. Over the years they have created a number of institutions that, taken together, cater to virtually every aspect of an individual's life, fulfilling the needs of the mind, body and soul. In addition, they settled with their families in Zanzibar early on. This stands in contrast with early Hindu traders who left their families in India.[6]

For centuries, South Asia and East Africa have been linked economically and culturally. The craftsmanship seen in Zanzibari doors has South Asian origins. The Indian Siddhis have African origins, and the Swahili language contains many South Asian

MAP 2 ETHNIC DISTRIBUTION OF ASIAN COMMUNITIES IN STONETOWN, ZANZIBAR

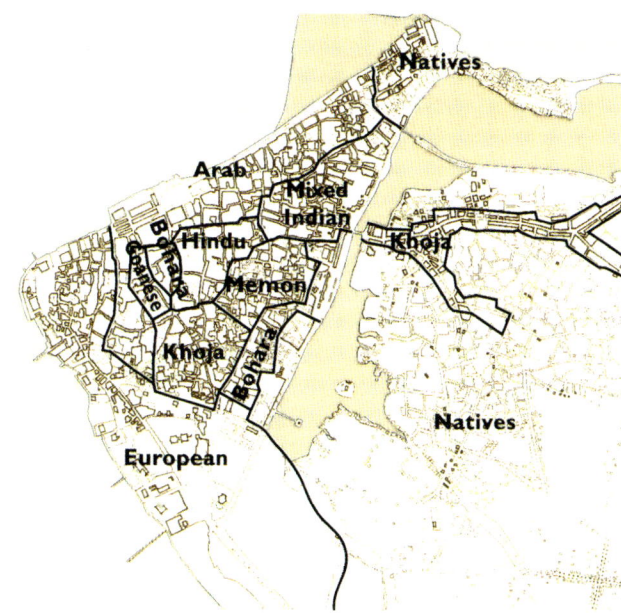

Reproduced from:

A. Sheriff, *Historical Zanzibar, Romance of the Ages*, Zanzibar 1995.

(Gujarati) words. In fact, the Indian Ocean region may be seen as a geographical area connected by the Indian Ocean, rather than divided by it. The Karimjees played a key role in linking East Africa with South Asia. First they arrived as migrants from India in Zanzibar and eventually settled there. Second, they continued their profession as merchants and traded all kinds of goods between East Africa and South Asia. In this chapter we will show that this migration was much more than the result of 'push and pull' factors. Rather, it was a process in which risk had to be calculated, in which the perilous journeys across the seas were just one major factor. In addition, their knowledge of the African and Indian market had to be excellent if they were to make a profit. However, reliable information was extremely scarce.

The British medical doctor James Christie visited Zanzibar regularly between 1821 and 1872. He was especially interested in the causes and consequences of the cholera epidemics in the area. He wrote in 1876 about the Bohras in Zanzibar:

"They are less numerous than the Khojas, and are similarly occupied in commerce (…). The Bahoras [sic] are a highly respectable class of people, and quietly pursue their own avocations without interfering with anyone else. They are rigid Muslims, but worship in their own mosque, and have no connections with other Mohammedan sects. They have their peculiar dress, and are the only class in Zanzibar, with the exception of the Persians, who wear a kind of trousers." [7]

This again reflects the image of the Bohras as a small, respected, self-contained community. Most South Asian migrants arrived in East Africa with little or no money. However, they had access to capital through community networks. Only a few families arrived with significant amounts of capital. It is plausible that Jivanjee did not arrive with a substantial amount of capital. But his father's connection with Jairam Sewji suggests that he was at least looked after and received moral support. The British representative in Zanzibar, Sir Bartle Frere, made the following observation in 1873:

"Arriving at his future scene of business with little beyond credentials of his fellow caste men, after perhaps a brief apprenticeship in some older firms, he starts a shop of his own with goods advanced on credit by some large house, and after a few years, when he has made a little money, generally returns home to marry, to make fresh business connections, and then comes back to Africa to repeat, on a large scale." [8]

This may have been the pattern followed by Jivanjee. We know, for example, that he arrived in Zanzibar in 1818, and formally established his own company in 1825. In the second half of the 19th century, European traders and officials realised that most of the trade in Zanzibar and along the East African coast was in the hands of South Asians.

Major General C.P. Rigby wrote in the 1860s:

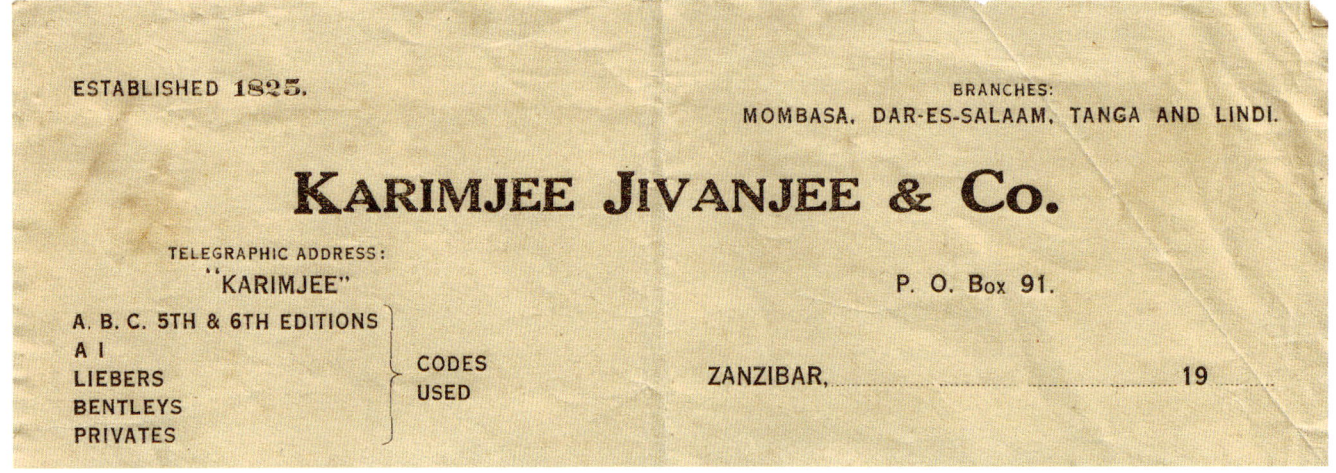

Letterhead from 1921 referring to the establishement of Karimjee Jivanjee & Co. in 1825.

CHAPTER 2 • CONNECTING ASIA AND AFRICA

"Nearly the whole of the local trade of Zanzibar is in the hands of British Indian Subjects, viz. Banyans, Khojas, and Bhoras, some who are very wealthy. The American, French and German merchants conduct nearly all their business through these natives of India, who would however much prefer trading with English merchants, as they know that all the disputes arising would then be settled by the British Consul and according to the same law for both parties." [9]

This is indeed the general migration pattern followed by many South Asian traders. This pattern leaves open the option to return to India for those who were unable to find a job or who were not successful in business. Others would move on to southern Africa to try their luck there. Therefore, India served as a reservoir of new recruits as well as a safety net for those who did not make it in Africa. In the case of the Karimjees, the option to return disappeared gradually. Jivanjee had started a flourishing trading firm and he was succeeded by his four sons: Ebrahimjee, Esmailjee, Pirbhai and Karimjee Jivanjee. One family tree reveals one daughter, Fatamben, but there is no additional information about her. The eldest son Ebrahimjee may have died early, because his name disappeared from the records in the 1850s.[10]

In 1861 the then three surviving brothers, Esmailjee, Pirbhai and the youngest brother Karimjee, separated their business interests. Whether the separation was a practical one or due to disagreements within the family remains unclear. The two eldest sons, Esmailjee and Pirbhai, continued the family's business in Zanzibar. However, following the death of Pirbhai the company was renamed the 'Esmailjee Jivanjee Company'. It developed a wide range of businesses, such as being a major importer of grain and holding the agency for kerosene in East Africa.[11] Esmailjee eventually migrated in 1880 to Mombasa and was among the first Bohras to settle there. Like many of his South Asian contemporaries, he had set up his business in East Africa, but his longing for India remained. It is likely that he retired in Mandvi. It is certain that he left a building to charity, which was to be used as a girl's school in Mandvi in 1902. This is probably one of the first charitable gifts in North West India to have been donated by an Asian African.

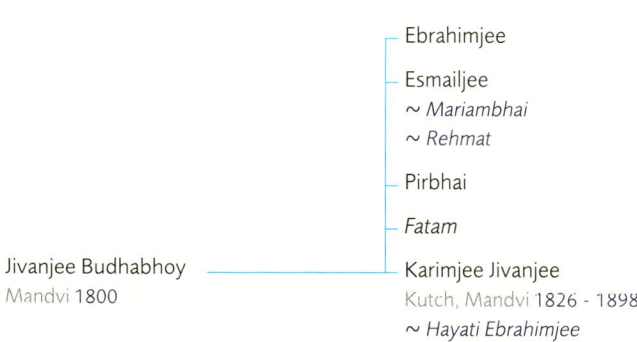

Jivanjee Budhabhoy
Mandvi 1800

- Ebrahimjee
- Esmailjee
  ~ *Mariambhai*
  ~ *Rehmat*
- Pirbhai
- *Fatam*
- Karimjee Jivanjee
  Kutch, Mandvi 1826 - 1898
  ~ *Hayati Ebrahimjee*

Alibhai Karimjee Jivanjee
Zanzibar 1851 - 1883 Zanzibar
~ *Fatema Jafferjee* † 1925

25

A beautifully designed two-storey building in Mandvi. The plain front door does not reflect its original design, as it was replaced after the Gujurat earthquake in 2000. Karimjee Jivanjee's older brother Esmailjee sponsored the building. From a Karimjee family album.

This plaque is one of the earliest physical pieces of evidence of the relationship between Mandvi, the Karimjees and East Africa. It was not replaced after the building was reconstructed following the Gujurat earthquake in 2000. Photo obtained through a local contact.

A HOUSE IN INDIA

The front doors of the houses in the streets of Mandvi are smaller and simpler than the well-known Zanzibari doors, but they are built in a similar style. It is easy to imagine that the craftsmen, who once built the Zanzibari doors, originally came from this area. One of the most intriguing buildings related to the family's history here is the building at the entrance of the Timba Falia in the old part of the town. Esmailjee Jivanjee, Karimjee Jivanjee's older brother, sponsored this building to be used as a girl's school. There used to be a plaque near its entrance gate, reading as follows:

> "Sheth Ismailjee Jivanjee & Company Jagbarwala [meaning 'from Zanzibar'] has donated this building in the memory of their late father Sheth Ismailjee Jivanjee to the Dawoodi Bohra Jamat for the purpose of Madrassa Ismalia – dated 27th October 1902."

It is possible that the houses in the street opposite the building used to belong to Esmailjee Jivanjee. Some of the elderly tenants remember that they had to pay rent to a middleman related to the Jivanjees. It is unclear, however, what happened to his inheritance after his death. Thus after the Jivanjee brothers separated and continued to do business on their own accounts, Esmaijee must have gone back to Mandvi to maintain some connection with their place of origin. Perhaps he went back to retire in Mandvi. In fact, this would fit the more general migration pattern where elderly members of the community preferred to retire in their place of birth.

CHAPTER 2 · CONNECTING ASIA AND AFRICA

The youngest brother Karimjee Jivanjee (1826 - 1898) set up his own business in Zanzibar under the name of Karimjee Jivanjee & Co. In the late 19th century, he was exporting commodities such as ivory, copra, groundnuts, cereals, beeswax and cloves from Zanzibar and the East African mainland to India. Eventually, the Karimjee Jivanjee firm had developed into a truly international company. It shipped directly to Europe, where it had its own buying and selling agents. In addition, business was conducted with Mauritius, Madagascar, and the Seychelles as well as with India and Ceylon (now Sri Lanka). The Karimjees, like most South Asians, were not involved in either the slave trade or the inland caravan trade. This was left to the Arabs, who were the key group of traders to explore the African interiors.[12]

Karimjee Jivanjee also looked after the family affairs, most importantly, the marriage of his son Alibhai. In those days, most Bohra brides were recruited from India. So, one day in the late 1860s, he went to India to arrange the marriage of his only son. After Karimjee Jivanjee had settled his family affairs in India, he apparently invested all he had in goods in India with the intention of selling them in Zanzibar. Unfortunately, he lost his entire investment as the cargo had to be jettisoned during a violent storm on the return journey. He arrived in Zanzibar penniless and probably had debts with some of his fellow community members in Zanzibar. However, the Karimjees had worked to acquire a good name and Jivanjee was determined to maintain that valuable asset within the community. Most likely he had to work for some of his creditors to repay his debts. Nonetheless, he was able to expand his own business in a comparatively short period of time. This was due to his tenacity and patience as well as a system of 'trust' within the Bohra community, in which reliable and trustworthy members of the community were able to take out loans on relatively favourable terms.[13]

Karimjee Jivanjee's son, Alibhai, died in 1885 at an early age of 32. This must have been a great loss to him. Not only because he was his only son and preferred successor, but also because Alibhai left five very young children, four sons and a daughter: Abdulhuscin, Hassanali, Mohamedali, Yusufali and his daughter Jenambai. Moreover, Alibhai's eldest son Abdulhusein died in 1892 at just 22. This made it unusually challenging to find a successor for Karimjee Jivanjee & Co.

The three surviving grandsons were bright but still very young (between 10-20 years) and inexperienced. Karimjee had already built a business network that so impressive that it was doubtful whether they would be able to continue the existing trading activities. Jivanjee had no other choice, but to continue the family business on his own. He must have anticipated the difficulties concerning the continuation of the firm. In all probability, he invited his grandsons to learn the business 'on the job' at an early age. Karimjee Jivanjee died in 1898. Although they were young, the Jivanjees' grandsons were able to continue the family business successfully.[14] The second eldest son, Hassanali Alibhai Karimjee (1872 - 1918) became the senior partner of the firm at the age of 26.

In the late 19th century, the Karimjees lived next door to each other on Hurumzi Street in Zanzibar. These houses were kept in the family until the beginning of the 20th century. The houses are still there and have been recently incorporated into the 236 Hurumzi Hotel (formerly the well-known Emerson and Green Hotel). It is a large three-storey building in the centre of Stone Town. The famous Indian trader Tharia Thopan originally built the house in the mid-19th century. The Karimjees probably bought the house in the last quarter. Perhaps it was Karimjee Jivanjee who bought the house from Tharia Thopan. This remains a matter of speculation. Nevertheless, he stayed with his wife Hayati and their son Alibhai (1851 - 1883) in the Hurumzi house while in Zanzibar. Alibhai's wife Fatema Jafferjee is still known in the family to have run that household efficiently.

Fatema Jafferjee Karimjee Jivanjee around 1920. She was the mother of Hassanali, Mohamedali and Yusufali. She foresaw the future of the Karimjee family as plantation barons.

Alibhai's son Hassanali died in early 1918. His wife Zainab raised their child (Tayabali) here, but she also looked after the children of others who moved elsewhere.[15] This shows the flexibility offered by an extended family, which allows the young and ambitious family members to travel, expand business elsewhere and leave their spouses and children behind in a secure family environment.

With several family members having suddenly died at an early age, the family was looking for explanations. In this period the family started to believe some ancient myths. Some of them are still shared today. Fatema Jafferjee (Alibhai's wife) remembered a story told by her mother that women should not wear diamonds, as this would bring bad luck to the family. This story is still told in the family. Therefore, diamonds were not given as a wedding present or wedding gift in the Karimjee Jivanjee family. In addition, even now, some of the Karimjee men will not buy

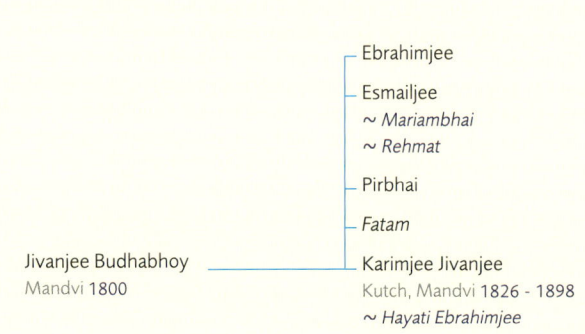

CHAPTER 2 · CONNECTING ASIA AND AFRICA

diamonds for their wives. This myth may have its origin in the fact that diamonds are indivisible. This could cause difficulties if families split up or if an inheritance needed to be distributed.

A second myth that surfaced in this period was that one should not breed a peacock in the shamba (the yard beyond the house). A peacock would bring 'ego' in the family. Egos will eventually fight and combat each other, which would harm the family business. A third myth that arose was the rule that 'one should not entertain royalty.' This may have been part of a bigger idea among business families that it is unwise to participate in politics, whereas it is often wiser – from a business perspective – to remain 'neutral'. These myths never played a dominant role in daily affairs, but do shows some of the dilemmas that large and well-off business families had to contend with.[16] The Karimjee Jivanjee family was very well able to do so.

Interestingly, the same Fatema Jafferjee Karimjee Jivanjee is said to have foreseen the Karimjees' shift towards agriculture and estates. In a dream she saw enormous plains on which long rows of green plants (tea? sisal?) were growing that had to be harvested. This dream eventually materialised in the next chapter of the expansion of the Karimjee empire.

The migration of the Karimjees was part of a larger process of economic and cultural interaction in the Indian Ocean Region. Nevertheless, the number of Bohra migrants in Zanzibar remained small. In the last two decades of the 19th century, it became clear that the Karimjees were not migrants, but settlers in Zanzibar. They had established their business successfully in Zanzibar, despite some drawbacks. Karimjee Jivanjee's son Alibhai was born, raised, and buried in Zanzibar. His four grandchildren were born, raised and buried in Zanzibar. Fatema dreamt of a future in East Africa. In other words, Africa had become their home, their future.

Alibhai Karimjee Jivanjee
Zanzibar 1851 - 1883 Zanzibar
~ Fatema Jafferjee † 1925

1. Abdulhussein Karimjee Jivanjee
Zanzibar 1870 - 1892 Zanzibar
~ Amtulla Ali Sethwala

2. Hassanali Karimjee Jivanjee
Zanzibar 1872 - 1918 Zanzibar
~ Zainab Noorbhai
Karachi 1872 - 1956 Karachi

3. Mohamedali Karimjee Jivanjee
Zanzibar 1876 - 1940 Zanzibar
~ Ratan Moosajee † 1912
~ Fatam Mohamedbhai
~ Namat Esmailji
~ Amtulla Noorbhai Jeevanjee
   1889-1944

4. Sir Yusufali Karimjee Jivanjee
Zanzibar 1882 - 1966 Zanzibar
~ Ratan Jafferjee † 1911
~ Sukan Zamindar
~ Lady Banoo Jivanjee née
   Katsuko Enomoto
   1905 - 1978 Osaka

5. Jenam † 1919
~ Mohamedali E. Jivanjee
~ Yusufali A. Lukmanji

Alibhai Karimjee Jivanjee.

Hassanali Karimjee Jivanjee.

Fatema Jafferjee, wife of Alibhai.

FAMILY GRAVES

The Bohra graveyard in Zanzibar (near to Mnazi Mmoja) has the oldest Bohra tombstones on the island. Among those who were buried in Zanzibar, we find Alibhai Karimjee (1851 - 1883) and his wife Fatema (died, 1925). Alibhai's sons, Hassanali (1872 - 1918) and Mohamedali (1876 - 1940) were buried here as well. Note that the inscriptions are predominantly in Arabic and Gujarati. It was only during Mohamedali's generation that Arabic was replaced by English. Sir Yusufali's wives Sukan and Ratan were also buried here, as well as Safia Mohamedali Karimjee (1908 - 1929), the third child of Mohamedali. Unfortunately, we do not know where the founding father Karimjee Jivanjee (1826 - 1898) was buried. If he went back to Mandvi to retire, like his older brother, his tombstone was probably demolished after the renovations of the Bohra graveyard close to the Mosque in 2000.

Mohamedali Alibhai Karimjee Jivanjee.

Safia Karimjee, daughter of Mohamedali.

Ratan Moosajee, wife of Mohamedali.

Sukan, wife of Yusufali.

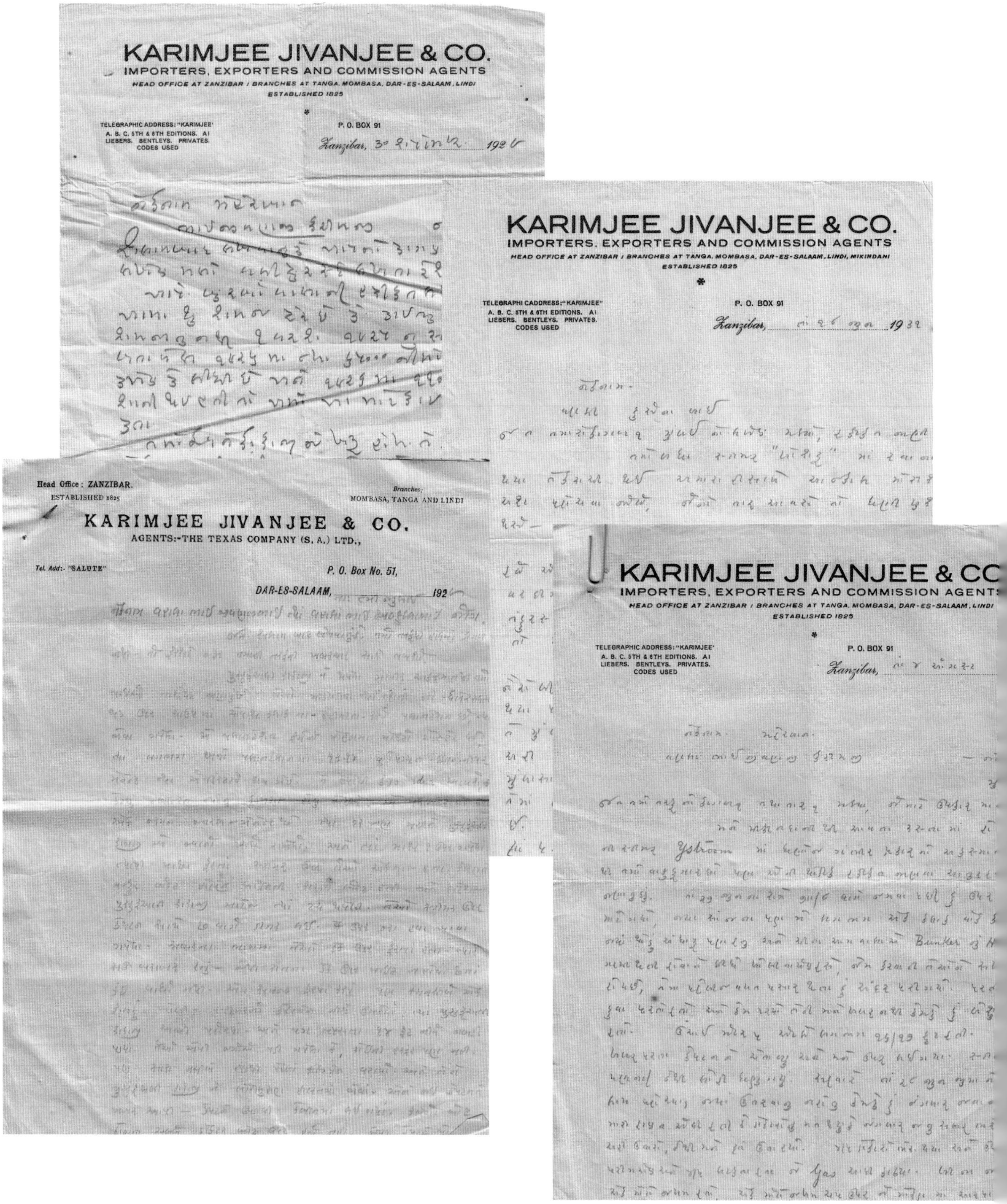
KARIMJEE JIVANJEE & CO.
IMPORTERS, EXPORTERS AND COMMISSION AGENTS
HEAD OFFICE AT ZANZIBAR / BRANCHES AT TANGA, MOMBASA, DAR-ES-SALAAM, LINDI
ESTABLISHED 1825
TELEGRAPHIC ADDRESS: "KARIMJEE"
A. B. C. 5TH & 6TH EDITIONS. A1
LIEBERS. BENTLEYS. PRIVATES.
CODES USED
P. O. BOX 91
Zanzibar, 192

KARIMJEE JIVANJEE & CO.
IMPORTERS, EXPORTERS AND COMMISSION AGENTS
HEAD OFFICE AT ZANZIBAR / BRANCHES AT TANGA, MOMBASA, DAR-ES-SALAAM, LINDI, MIKINDANI
ESTABLISHED 1825
TELEGRAPHI CADDRESS: "KARIMJEE"
A. B. C. 5TH & 6TH EDITIONS. A1
LIEBERS. BENTLEYS. PRIVATES.
CODES USED
P. O. BOX 91
Zanzibar, 193

Head Office: ZANZIBAR.
ESTABLISHED 1825
Branches:
MOMBASA, TANGA AND LINDI
KARIMJEE JIVANJEE & CO.
AGENTS:-THE TEXAS COMPANY (S. A.) LTD.,
Tel. Add:- "SALUTE"
P. O. Box No. 51,
DAR-ES-SALAAM, 192

KARIMJEE JIVANJEE & CO
IMPORTERS, EXPORTERS AND COMMISSION AGENTS
HEAD OFFICE AT ZANZIBAR / BRANCHES AT TANGA, MOMBASA, DAR-ES-SALAAM, LINDI
ESTABLISHED 1825
TELEGRAPHIC ADDRESS: "KARIMJEE"
A. B. C. 5TH & 6TH EDITIONS. A1
LIEBERS. BENTLEYS. PRIVATES.
CODES USED
P. O. BOX 91
Zanzibar,

CHAPTER 3

The making of a trading empire 1880 - 1924

In the late 19th century and early 20th century, three major developments shaped the history of the Karimjee Jivanjee family. First, the arrival of more and more Europeans opened up trade with Europe. Second, Tanganyika became a more stable political economy. The legislative order turned out to be more predictable, thereby clearing the way for further investment and expansion. Last but not least, the three great Karimjee tycoons took advantage of these developments and directed the family to a new level of wealth, political ambitions and charity.

Between 1880 - 1920, political power in East Africa was mainly divided between the Sultan of Oman, the British and the Germans. The Omani ruler Seyyid Said had moved his capital from Oman to Zanzibar in 1832. Many South Asian traders and financiers in Oman followed the Sultan Seyyid Said to Zanzibar. The Sultan appointed the Indian Jairam Sewji as the customs collector. And, as we saw in Chapter one, it was Jairam who had approached Buddhabhoy earlier on to explore the opportunities in Zanzibar. A commercial treaty in 1839 between Said and Britain guaranteed British subjects the freedom to enter Zanzibar and to reside and engage in trade within the Sultan's dominion. The establishment of a British consulate in Zanzibar further encouraged Indians to settle there because of the sense of security and the expectation of protection in their dealings with the Arab aristocracy. Later, the British sphere of influence spanned much of Kenya and Uganda, while the Germans had gained control of Tanganyika. Over the course of time, the influence of the Sultan of Oman declined, with Zanzibar becoming a British protectorate in 1890.

Tanganyika became a British protectorate in 1919, after the Germans lost the First World War. Officially this was just a mandate issued by the United Nations, but in practice the British were in charge of the region. They were now in political control of Uganda, Kenya, Tanganyika and Zanzibar. In other words, the region developed from being ruled by different political powers to being run by a more centralised government from the Colonial Office in London. The Colonial Office kept regional boundaries intact for administrative reasons.

In the period between 1880 and 1920, the Karimjee family business came to an important crossroads. In the last chapters we have seen that Karimjee Jivanjee effectively managed the trading company until his death in 1898. His four bright grandsons managed to keep the company running, despite being quite young: Abdulhusein (1870 - 1892), Hassanali (1872 - 1918), Mohamedali (1876 - 1940) and Yusufali (1882 - 1966). In true 'family business' fashion, the Karimjee brothers divided the main responsibilities among the partners of the firm. The eldest grandson died early. Therefore it was the second eldest son, Hassanali, who became the family's oldest member and looked after the financial affairs of the company in Zanzibar. The third son, Mohamedali, managed the coastal trading business and the general department, while the youngest son, Yusufali, was responsible for the English and South and East Asian part of

Various business letters in Gujarati in the 1920s.

the business. After a while, each of the sons developed his own career in business as well as in public life.[17]

Mohamedali Karimjee developed the 'head office' in Zanzibar into a reliable trading partner for an incredible number of European companies. He managed the important international trading licences that the Karimjees acquired. His younger brother Yusufali became the 'outbound manager and explorer'. He travelled from Zanzibar to Japan and Europe to explore new markets and trades. Eventually, his motto 'wealth imposes obligations' became practice, as he increasingly became involved in charities. He was ultimately knighted for his contributions in East Africa. Their nephew Tayabali Karimjee developed a career in the family business, politics and charities. He wrote himself into Zanzibari history as a member of the Legislative Council. Additionally, he was knighted for his public and charitable contributions to the Zanzibari community.

At this stage, the Karimjee Jivanjee Company was still a trading company, trading in a wide range of products. The majority of trading was in agricultural products and textiles. Goods were imported from a wide range of countries, including the UK, Germany and India and the Far East. East African agricultural products were exported to the same countries, as well as Mauritius, the Seychelles, and Ceylon. The company owned many dhows, which were used for the coastal trade, especially with Pemba, Tanga, Dar es Salaam, Bagamoyo, Kilwa, Lindi, Mikindani, Mombasa and Lamu. The Karimjees developed their own trading agencies in most of these places.

A famous and important trading directory published in 1909 summarises the business activities of Karimjee Jivanjee & Co. as follows:

"Their principal imports are Manchester cotton goods; sugar from Austria, Germany and Russia; rice from India; tea and coffee, beads (Bohemian and Viennese); metal – especially galvanised iron from Birmingham; oil, paints, nails and all kinds of merchandise except hams and bacon which are prohibited owing to their religion. Exports (…) local produce, such as cloves, copra, hides, beeswax, rubber, chillies, all kinds of shells, groundnuts and East African produce. They have a certificate of merit for cloves awarded at the Zanzibar Exhibition of 1905." [18]

At the turn of the century, an increasing number of European and American companies were looking for a reliable partner to organise their exports. Numerous companies established overseas realised that the Karimjees were the ones they had to deal with in East Africa. Thus, when foreign traders and companies wished to deal with the Karimjees, they came to pay a visit to the Karimjee office. Mohamedali and Hassanali made sure that they were able to receive the foreign visitors, as they were the major and constant factor in the family business in Zanzibar. Where the western companies were looking for a reliable partner in East Africa, the Karimjees had to find out whether these foreign companies were trustworthy. Often, the question was whether these companies were seeking a long-term partnership or just looking for 'a quick buck'. For them, East Africa was an alien, strange market and a big adventure. Mohamedali and Hassanali had to determine whether there was a market in East Africa for the products offered, and if so, whether the quality of the products would be suitable for the East African climate and circumstances. Thus, they collected all the available

This is a page taken from an important trading directory, compiled by the British Colonial Official Somerset Playne in the early 1900s. He travelled across the British Empire to locate the most important local businesses. His famous business directories provided a wealth of information to Europeans and others for finding various types of firms, businesses and traders across the globe. The directory related to East Africa was entitled: East Africa (British). Its History, People, Commerce, Industries, and Resources, published by the Foreign and Colonial Compiling and Publishing Company, 1909, pp. 420-423.

KARIMJEE JIVANJEE AND CO.

Y. A. KARIMJEE.   A PILE OF CLOVES.   H. A. KARIMJEE.
M. A. KARIMJEE.   THE RESIDENCE.   CERTIFICATE OF MERIT FOR CLOVES.

information, the important data and organised the 'facts and figures' in such a way that the family was able to make the right decisions. In addition, during his numerous travels, Yusufali was able to collect information from Europe. His knowledge of the European market and cuture helped the Karimjees to make the right decisions. Eventually, the Karimjees acquired trading licenses for about 40-50 different European and American companies. Depending on their expectations, they negotiated various trading deals. Some articles, goods and foodstuffs were sold at a small fee, others were given in consignment, but most of them were probably bought wholesale, leaving the Karimjee Trading Company with the best possible profit margin.

Over time, Karimjee Jivanjee & Co. acquired numerous trading licenses in a wide range of products in East Africa. These

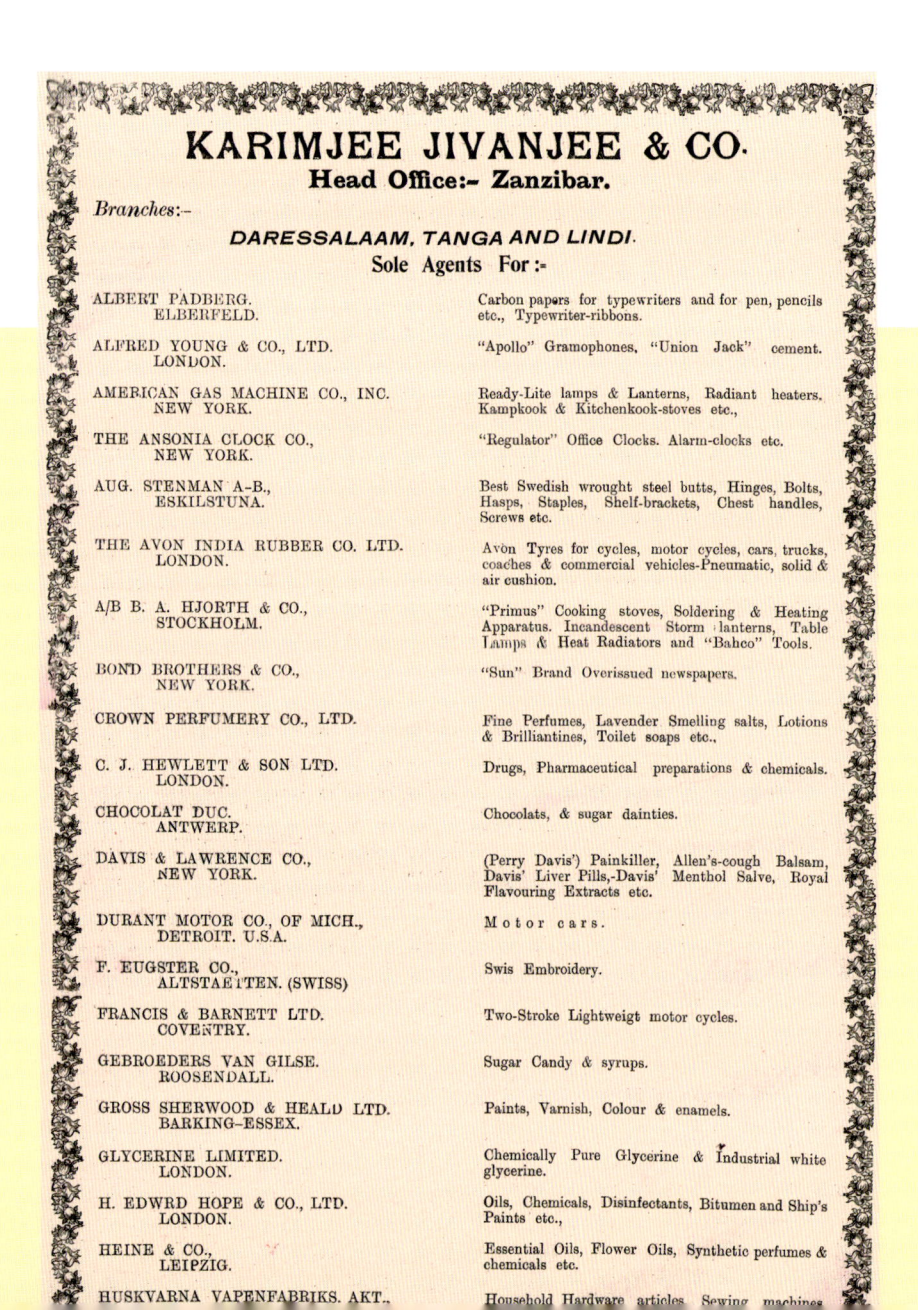

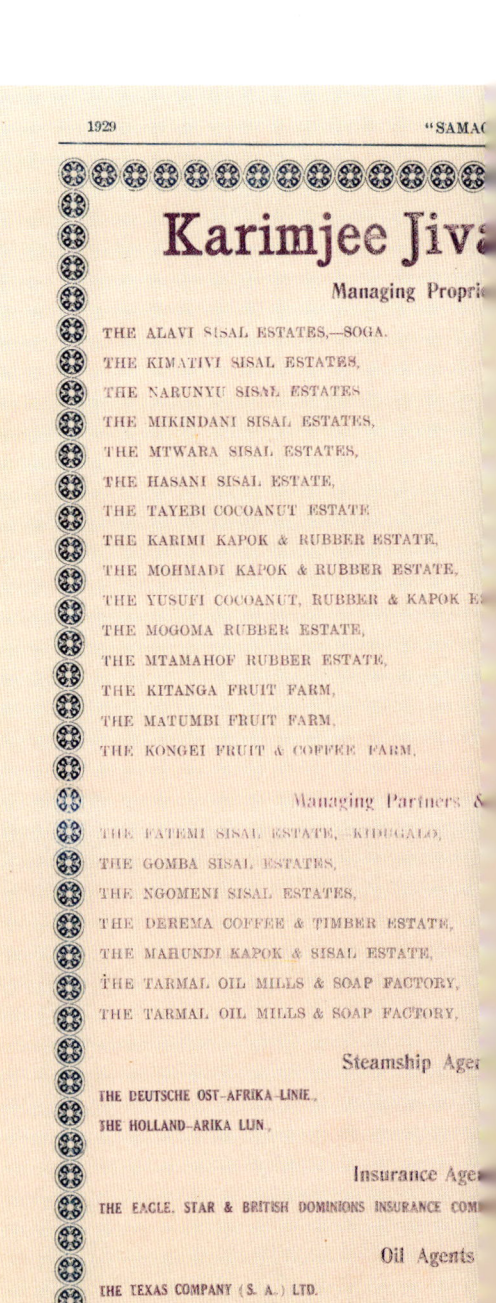

KARIMJEE JIVANJEE & CO.
Head Office:- Zanzibar.

Branches:-

DARESSALAAM, TANGA AND LINDI.

Sole Agents For :-

ALBERT PADBERG. ELBERFELD.	Carbon papers for typewriters and for pen, pencils etc., Typewriter-ribbons.
ALFRED YOUNG & CO., LTD. LONDON.	"Apollo" Gramophones, "Union Jack" cement.
AMERICAN GAS MACHINE CO., INC. NEW YORK.	Ready-Lite lamps & Lanterns, Radiant heaters. Kampkook & Kitchenkook-stoves etc.,
THE ANSONIA CLOCK CO., NEW YORK.	"Regulator" Office Clocks. Alarm-clocks etc.
AUG. STENMAN A-B., ESKILSTUNA.	Best Swedish wrought steel butts, Hinges, Bolts, Hasps, Staples, Shelf-brackets, Chest handles, Screws etc.
THE AVON INDIA RUBBER CO. LTD. LONDON.	Avon Tyres for cycles, motor cycles, cars, trucks, coaches & commercial vehicles-Pneumatic, solid & air cushion.
A/B B. A. HJORTH & CO., STOCKHOLM.	"Primus" Cooking stoves, Soldering & Heating Apparatus. Incandescent Storm lanterns, Table Lamps & Heat Radiators and "Bahco" Tools.
BOND BROTHERS & CO., NEW YORK.	"Sun" Brand Overissued newspapers.
CROWN PERFUMERY CO., LTD.	Fine Perfumes, Lavender Smelling salts, Lotions & Brilliantines, Toilet soaps etc.,
C. J. HEWLETT & SON LTD. LONDON.	Drugs, Pharmaceutical preparations & chemicals.
CHOCOLAT DUC. ANTWERP.	Chocolates, & sugar dainties.
DAVIS & LAWRENCE CO., NEW YORK.	(Perry Davis') Painkiller, Allen's-cough Balsam, Davis' Liver Pills,-Davis' Menthol Salve, Royal Flavouring Extracts etc.
DURANT MOTOR CO., OF MICH., DETROIT. U.S.A.	Motor cars.
F. EUGSTER CO., ALTSTAETTEN. (SWISS)	Swis Embroidery.
FRANCIS & BARNETT LTD. COVENTRY.	Two-Stroke Lightweigt motor cycles.
GEBROEDERS VAN GILSE. ROOSENDALL.	Sugar Candy & syrups.
GROSS SHERWOOD & HEALD LTD. BARKING-ESSEX.	Paints, Varnish, Colour & enamels.
GLYCERINE LIMITED. LONDON.	Chemically Pure Glycerine & Industrial white glycerine.
H. EDWRD HOPE & CO., LTD. LONDON.	Oils, Chemicals, Disinfectants, Bitumen and Ship's Paints etc.,
HEINE & CO., LEIPZIG.	Essential Oils, Flower Oils, Synthetic perfumes & chemicals etc.
HUSKVARNA VAPENFABRIKS. AKT.	Household Hardware articles, Sewing machines

---

1929 "SAMAC

Karimjee Jiva

Managing Propri

- THE ALAVI SISAL ESTATES,—SOGA.
- THE KIMATIVI SISAL ESTATES,
- THE NARUNYU SISAL ESTATES
- THE MIKINDANI SISAL ESTATES,
- THE MTWARA SISAL ESTATES,
- THE HASANI SISAL ESTATE,
- THE TAYEBI COCOANUT ESTATE
- THE KARIMI KAPOK & RUBBER ESTATE,
- THE MOHMADI KAPOK & RUBBER ESTATE,
- THE YUSUFI COCOANUT, RUBBER & KAPOK E
- THE MOGOMA RUBBER ESTATE,
- THE MTAMAHOF RUBBER ESTATE,
- THE KITANGA FRUIT FARM,
- THE MATUMBI FRUIT FARM,
- THE KONGEI FRUIT & COFFEE FARM,

Managing Partners &

- THE FATEMI SISAL ESTATE,—KIDUGALO,
- THE GOMBA SISAL ESTATES,
- THE NGOMENI SISAL ESTATES,
- THE DEREMA COFFEE & TIMBER ESTATE,
- THE MAHUNDI KAPOK & SISAL ESTATE,
- THE TARMAL OIL MILLS & SOAP FACTORY,
- THE TARMAL OIL MILLS & SOAP FACTORY,

Steamship Age

- THE DEUTSCHE OST-AFRIKA-LINIE,
- THE HOLLAND-AFRIKA LIJN,

Insurance Age

- THE EAGLE, STAR & BRITISH DOMINIONS INSURANCE COM

Oil Agents

- THE TEXAS COMPANY (S. A.) LTD.

CHAPTER 3 · THE MAKING OF A TRADING EMPIRE, 1880 - 1924

included licenses for Singer Sewing Machines, Michelin (rubber tyres), Raleigh bicycles, Texas Company (oil products), the German East Africa Line and the Holland Africa line (shipment of passengers and goods). In short, the business of exploiting licenses was in good hands with the Karimjees. They were among the very few Asians in East Africa who were approached by Europeans and Americans to help them gain a foothold in the East African market.

Among these licenses were a few quite unusual ones, like the one for Ansonia Clock Co., from New York. This famous American clock and watchmaker had its economic heyday somewhere between 1890 - 1914 and, not surprisingly, it expanded to East Africa to supply the emerging group of planters and settlers. Even today, many of the antique clocks in

The Karimjees acquired numerous trading licenses to sell European and American products in East Africa. Many of them were mentioned in the "Samarchar" Silver Jubilee issue of 1929.

KARIMJEE JIVANJEE & CO.
Head Office:- Zanzibar.
BRANCHES:— **DARESSALAAM, TANGA AND LINDI.**
Sole Agents For :-

THE INDO-BURMA PETROLEUM CO., LTD. BOMBAY.	"Globelight" brand Mineral Wax candles.
INTERNATIONAL HARVESTER EXPORT COMPANY. CHICAGO. U.S.A.	Farm operating equipments, Motor Trucks Motor Busses, Industrial Tractors etc.,
JOHANN FABER A. G. NUREMBERG.	"Taj Mahal" "Golden" Rod blacklead, and "Postograph" Copying pencils, Pencil sharpeners, erasers etc.,
JOHN GRAY & CO., LTD. GLASGOW.	Jams, Jellies, Marmalade, chocolats, Caramels etc.,
JOHN STEPHENS, SON & CO., GLOUCESTER.	Pickles, Sauces, Jams, Marmalade, Candied peels-bottled fruits & malt vinegar.
JOSEPH CROSFIELD & SONS LTD., WARRINGTON.	Powdered Caustic Soda, Silicate of Soda, and 'Egg' brand Waterglass.
JOHN BIRCH & CO., LTD. LONDON.	"Robson" Crudel Oil Engines & Semi-Diesel Oil, Engines.
KARL LENDENMAN. REHETOBEL.	Swiss Embroidery.
KELVINATOR SALES CORPORATION. DETROIT. MICH.	Electric Refrigerators etc.,
LOUIS FUNEL. CANNET-CANNES.	Essence of Chypre & other perfumes,
N. V. ENFA. VENLO.	Envelopes & fancy stationery.
NETHERLANDS MARGARINE CO., LTD. LONDON.	Vegetable Ghee, Soaps etc.,
NASH MOTORS CO., KENOSHA.	Motor cars.
NADIRSHAW PRINTER & CO., BOMBAY.	Godrej's Toilet Soaps.
THE NATIONAL RUBBER CO., LTD. LONDON.	Rubber Solid & crepe sheets, Motor Hood Fabri Canvas rubber shoes etc.
PLAISTOWE & CO., LTD. LONDON.	"Fulcreem" Toffee & Caramels, Pickles & Sauc Jams & Marmalade. Custard powders etc.,
PREST-O-LITE STORAGE BATTERY SALES CORP., NEW YORK.	Prest-O-Lite batteries for Motor trucks, busses taxicabs etc.,
REX RESEARCH CORPORATION TOLEDO. U.S.A.	Fly - Tox. Rat-Tox & hand-sprayers
THE RAYMOND-HADLEY CO. INC. NEW YORK.	Best grade "Orlando" Flour.
RABONE BROTHERS & Co., BIRMINGHAM.	Higgs Motors (Electric Motor Generator Sets)
ROYAL TYPEWRITER Co., INC. NEW YORK.	"Royal" Standard & Portable typewriters. Carb papers & typewriter ribbons etc.,
S. F. TURNER LTD. DUDLEY.	Brass & Iron Bedsteads. Fire & burglar saf
THE STANDARDISED DISINFECTANTS CO., LTD. LONDON.	"Brunolinum" wood preservative, "Jetalina" Black Varnish & Sanitary Fluids etc.,
S. A. VVE CHS LEON SCHMID & CIE., CHAUX-DE-FONDS.	"Roskopf" Pocket, & Wristlet Silver, Rolled G and Gold watches in fancy shapes & designs.
SABO EMBROIDERIES LTD. ST. GALL.	Swiss Embroidery.
SMEETS HERFST & CO., MAASSTRICHT.	Dutch China Glass & Earthenware.
UNITED STATES CHAIN & FORGING CO., NEW YORK.	McKay Tire & cross Chains for motor cars, trucks, e

East Africa come from this company, having found their way to various locations thanks to a trading licence with the Karimjees. Many of them still bear the Karimjee name as the company used to sell them under its own brand name 'Karimjee Jivanjee'.

Another important license was for Huskvarna Husqvarna, a Swedish company founded in 1689. Originally, it produced weapons, mainly muskets. Later it developed some of the world's best products in areas such as hunting weapons, bicycles, motorcycles, kitchen appliances and sewing machines. Interestingly, the Karimjees also acquired the trading license for Singer Sewing Machines. Thus they were in possession of the trading licenses for two competing companies. After the First World War, the Karimjees acquired licenses with Durant Motors (New York), Francis-Barnett & Co. (Coventry, England) and Nash Motors & Co. (Kenosha, Wisconsin, United States).

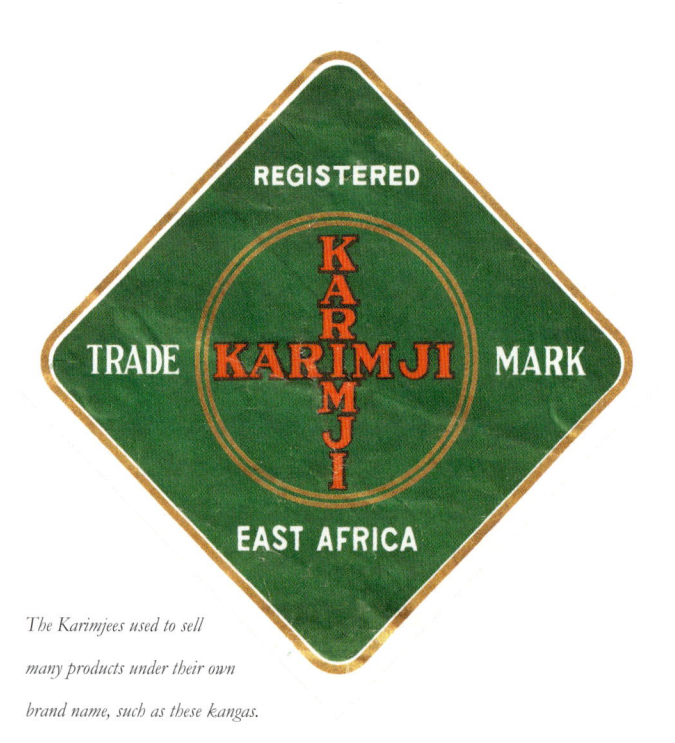

The Karimjees used to sell many products under their own brand name, such as these kangas.

Nevertheless, the Karimjees were not only agents for commodities, but they also represented insurance companies, like State Insurance Company of India, and Eagle Star Insurance Co. of Britain. However, not all the licenses were for luxury products for rich Asians and expatriates. A good example of this is the license for B.A. Hjorth and Co., which represented Primus Cooking Stoves. This may seem to be a trivial item, but in the days before electricity this was the principal mode of cooking. The Karimjees also supplied goods for lower income earners, like soap, pencils, kanga and other commodities. In addition, it may be interesting to note that many of these European and American companies firmly believed that Africa was destined to become the new America. The idea of a growing number of white settlers who eventually would bring about the continent's development was so strong that many companies wanted to gain a foothold in East Africa.

Mohamedali's responsibilities increased dramatically after his older brother Hassanali passed away in 1918. Now he was the oldest male member in the family and became the 'captain' of the family affairs. The first important issue Mohamedali settled was the position of Hassanali's only son, Tayabali, in the family and its business. Mohamedali must have realised that Tayabali, though still young, would sooner or later become very influential in the family business. He inherited one third of the shares, whereas the children of Mohamedali and Yusufali (eleven children each) were compelled to divide the shares among themselves. This would leave Tayabali with substantial influence in the company. Tayabali's marriage with Mohamedali's daughter Sugra probably redressed the balance of authority in the family. It was clear from the beginning that Tayabali would play his part in the family's business.

Mohamedali kept his responsibilities for the trade, the licences, warehouses and distribution of trades. Unfortunately, not much is known about his life in Zanzibar. He did not leave

CHAPTER 3 · THE MAKING OF A TRADING EMPIRE, 1880 - 1924

any letters, nor was he politically active. Most of the sources related to his life were archived in the Zanzibar office, which was nationalised during the Zanzibar revolution in 1964. The firm was growing rapidly and the Karimjees managed to expand in branch offices. They started with branch offices in Mombasa (1915), Dar es Salaam (1921), Tanga (1922), Lindi (1925) and Mikindani (1925). These branches were set up in true family business style. Mohamedali considered one of his or his brother Yusufali's children in his search for a capable manager to explore new opportunities elsewhere. In this fashion, Abdulla, Mohamedali's oldest son, started as a young boy in Dar es Salaam and was soon transferred to Tanga, whereas Abdulkarim, one of Yusufali's sons, remained responsible for the Dar es Salaam office. Sometimes, professional managers who had proven their abilities in the Zanzibar office – or elsewhere – were allowed to run the branches as well.

Whereas Mohamedali's and Tayabali's major responsibilities were in Zanzibar, Yusufali mainly became an outbound manager. He travelled extensively to expand the international Karimjee business network. He explored new markets, new products and new business families to trade with. In those days there was no reliable telephone service and very little access to telegraphy. Therefore, face-to-face interaction was extremely important. His ambitions surpassed many imaginable borders. Before the steamer became the most important mode of transport, Yusufali travelled by a sailing ship. He did not stop in India or Ceylon (three weeks travel). He visited Singapore as well (another four weeks) and then sailed from Japan to Zanzibar (more than 10 weeks travel) and from Zanzibar to Europe. Soon after he travelled by steamer, where he was often one of the only Asian passengers on board. He saw new trading opportunities wherever he went and his growing knowledge of international markets must have helped him to negotiate many profitable deals.

Amtulla Noorbhai Jeevanjee, 1889 - 1944.

Mohamedali and Amtulla.

3 Mohamedali Karimjee Jivanjee
Zanzibar 1876 -1940 Zanzibar
~ Ratan Moosajee † 1912
~ Fatam Mohamedbhai
~ Namat Esmailji
~ Amtulla Noorbhai Jeevanjee
1889 - 1944

N — Kulsum Karimjee
1920 Karachi
~ Esmail Jafferjee

N — Abdulla M. A. Karimjee OBE
Zanzibar 1899 - 1978 Sharjah
~ Sukan Y. Karimjee
Zanzibar 1903 - 1975 Karachi
~ Kianga Ranniger
Tanganyika 1910 - 1973 Spain

- **Hasan Karimjee** S
  Zanzibar 1918 - 1989 London
  ~ Zubeida H. G. M. Jivanjee
  Hyderabad 1923 - 1971 London
  Sind
  - **Nishat Karimjee**
    Bombay 1947
    ~ Jose Luis Garcia
    ~ Dante Carignano
    Argentina 1945
    - Valerio Carignano D
      Paris 1980
  - **Zeenat Karimjee**
    Bombay 1949 - 1978 London
  - **Mumtaz Karimjee**
    Bombay 1951

- **Fidahussein Karimjee** S
  Zanzibar 1920 - 1942 Jog Falls

- **Zehra Karimjee** S
  Zanzibar 1923
  ~ Hatim Noorani
  Karachi 1912 - 1975 Karachi
  - **Aziz Noorani**
    Bombay 1946
    ~ Rashida Lookmanjee
    - Alina Noorani
      London 1988
  - **Mustafa Noorani**
    Karachi 1948
    ~ Shameem Sachak
    Tanga 1948
    - Soraiya Noorani
      High Wycombe 1985
    - Asad Noorani
      High Wycombe 1988
  - **Ruby Noorani**
    Karachi 1951
    ~ Inayat Valliani
    - Aliya Valliani
      USA 1979
    - Nadia Valliani
      USA 1981
  - **Nafisa Noorani**
    Karachi 1956
    ~ Fahim Saleji
    Karachi 1957 - 1986 Boston
    - Zakir Saleji
      USA 1985

N — Lady Sugra Karimjee
Hyderabad 1902 - 1973 Karachi
Sind
~ Sir Tayabali Karimjee
Zanzibar 1897 - 1987 Karachi

N — Safia Karimjee
Zanzibar 1908 - 1929 Zanzibar

- **Dr Shokat A. Karimjee** S
  Zanzibar 1925 - 1980 London
  ~ Munira Barros Sa
  Goa 1924 - 2001 London
  - **Dr Shabnam Karimjee**
    Lakewood, Ohio 1952
    - Kamila Karimjee
      London 1995
  - **Azim Karimjee**
    Lakewood, Ohio 1953
    ~ Mitra Alam
    London 1957
    - Adnan Karimjee
      London 1999

A — Alibhai M. A. Karimjee
Mauritius 1912 - 1996 Mauritius
~ Shirin Karimjee
Zanzibar 1914 - 2002 Mauritius

- **Shameem Karimjee**
  Dar es Salaam 1942
  ~ Hussain Currimjee
  Mauritius 1934 - 1976 Mauritius
  - **Soraya Currimjee**
    Mauritius 1964
    ~ Norbert Verhalen
  - **Nishaat Currimjee**
    Mauritius 1971
    ~ Gilbert Sunglee
    Mauritius 1972

- **Mahmood Karimjee**
  Zanzibar 1945 - 1945 Zanzibar

- **Nazim Karimjee**
  Zanzibar 1948
  ~ Susanne Carol Taylor
  Brighton 1945
  - **Shariffa Karimjee**
    Nottingham 1974
    ~ Ian Wright
    Glasgow 1971
  - **Sakina Rehana Karimjee**
    Nottingham 1978

A — Adbulkader Karimjee
Zanzibar 1913 - 2005 Mauritius
~ Zohra G. Noorani
Karachi 1914

- **Yasmin Karimjee**
  Karachi 1944
- **Mohammed Iqbal Karimjee**
  Karachi 1948
  ~ Sharon Lesly Dunsmore
  Nottingham 1961
  ~ Pamela Joan Veich
  Birkenhead 1947
  - **Sasha Yasmin Karimjee** S
    Nottingham 1983
    - Sara Ann Karimjee
      Nottingham 2002
  - **Adam John Karimjee** S
    Nottingham 1985
- **Hilal Karimjee**
  London 1952

A — Akberhusein Karimjee
Zanzibar 1914 - 1922 Zanzibar

A — Adamali Karimjee
Zanzibar 1915 - 1961 Muheza
~ Zaibun Alavi
Karachi 1923

- **Latif Karimjee**
  Karachi 1948
  ~ Suraiya Esufally
  Colombo 1951
  - **Aina Karimjee**
    Colombo 1974
    ~ Anis Suterwalla
    London 1974
  - **Husein Karimjee**
    Colombo 1979
  - **Kumayl Karimjee**
    London 1990

A — Batul Karimjee
Zanzibar 1918 - 2002 Mauritius
~ Fazal Y. Karimjee
Zanzibar 1912 - 1992 Mauritius

- **Jameela Karimjee**
  Tanga 1952
  ~ Firoze Fakhri
  Calcutta 1947
  - Adam Fahkri
    Chicago 1975
  - Talib Fahkri
    Los Angeles 1981

A — Anver Ali Karimjee
Zanzibar 1922 - 2003 London
~ Christianne Von Lindenau
~ Rubab T. Sachak
Tanga 1930

- **Rehma Karimjee** *
  Bombay 1952
- **Safia Karimjee** R
  Tanga 1959
  ~ Mustan Ebrahimjee
  Nairobi 1957
  - Naeem Ebrahimjee
    London 1987
  - Anisah Ebrahimjee
    London 1990
- **Saleem Karimjee** R
  Zürich 1960
- **Arif Karimjee** R
  Karachi 1967
  ~ Fiona Burnside
  Croydon 1963
  - Zakariyah Karimjee
    Twickenham 1998
  - Haris Karimjee
    Bagshot 2000

A — Khatun Karimjee
Zanzibar 1922 - 1980 Manchester
~ Hamza A. Alavi
Karachi 1921-2003 Karachi

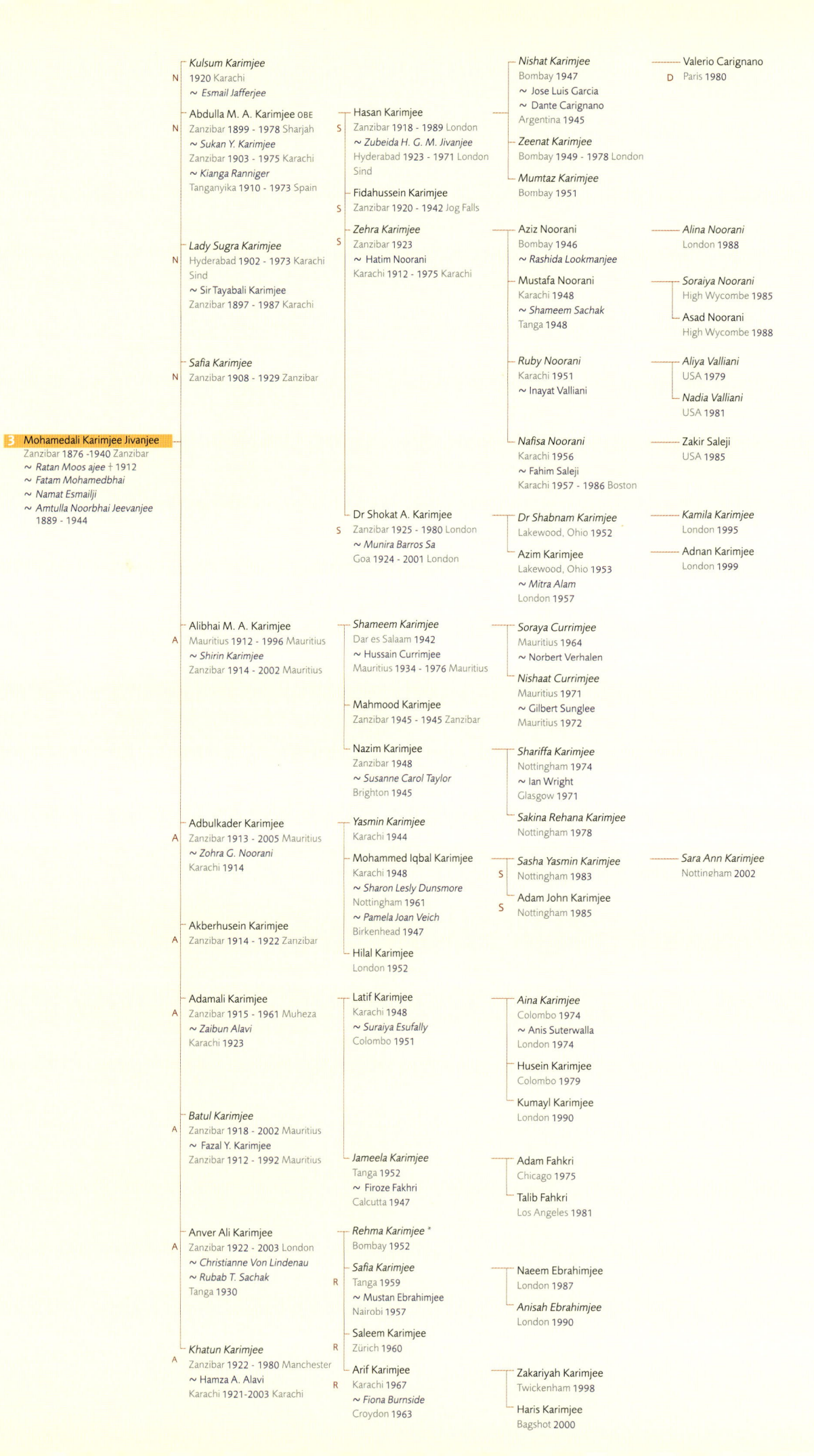

CHAPTER 3 · THE MAKING OF A TRADING EMPIRE, 1880 – 1924

Family picture of the Mohamedali line in 1930.

Back row (left to right): Anver, Khatun, Adam, Batul, and Abdulkader.

Seated (left to right): Sukan, Mohamedali, Rehmat (Amtulla's mother), Amtulla, Abdulla.

Front row (left to right): Fidahussein and Shokat (sons of Abdulla).

CHAPTER 3 · THE MAKING OF A TRADING EMPIRE, 1880 - 1924

Yusufali and Sukan with ten children, in 1930.
Back row (left to right); Fazal, Abdulkarim, Amir.
Seated (left to right); Shirin, Husseina, Sukan (Yusufali's wife), Yusufali, Sukan, Rubab.
Front row (left to right); Abid, Hatim, Zainab.

Children from his marriage with his first wife Ratan; Taher (not pictured), Sukan, Abdulkarim, Husseina, Rubab and Fazal.
Children from his marriage with his second wife Sukan; Shirin, Amir, Hatim, Zainab and Abid.

4 Sir Yusufali Karimjee Jivanjee
Zanzibar 1882 - 1966 Zanzibar
~ Ratan Jafferjee † 1911
~ Sukan Zamindar
~ Lady Banoo Jivanjee née Katsuko Enomoto
1905 - 1978 Osaka

R — Taher Y. A. Karimjee

Sukan Y. A. Karimjee
Zanzibar 1903 - 1975 Karachi
~ Abdulla M. A. Karimjee OBE
Zanzibar 1898 - 1978 Sharjah

R — Abdulkarim Y. A. Karimjee CBE
Zanzibar 1906 - 1977 London
~ Batul Noorbhai
Karachi 1911 - 1989 Karachi

- Ratan Karimjee
  † 1936 Dar es Salaam
  ~ Jabir Haji Khandwala
  Karachi 1930 - 1997 London

- *Rosemine Karimjee*
  Dar es Salaam 1939
  ~ Mustan A. Currimjee
  Zanzibar 1936

Huseina Karimjee
R Zanzibar 1908 - 2004 Mauritius
~ Abdulla Currimjee
Mauritius 1905 - 1977 Mauritius

- Carrim Currimjee
  Bombay 1931
  ~ Veena Shah
  Bombay 1933

  - Shama Currimjee
    Mauritius 1961
    ~ Nirvan Veerasamy
    Mauritius 1960

    - Lamia Veerasamy
      Toulouse 1989
    - Leila Veerasamy
      Toulouse 1993

  - Anil Currimjee
    Mauritius 1962
    ~ Natacha Nundlall
    Mauritius 1964

    - Zara Currimjee
      Mauritius 1991
    - Raza Currimjee
      Mauritius 1993
    - Naomi Currimjee
      Mauritius 1995

  - Salim Currimjee
    Mauritius 1963

- Mustan Currimjee
  Zanzibar 1936
  ~ Rosemine Karimjee
  Dar es Salaam 1939

  - Ashraf Currimjee
    Mauritius 1962
    ~ Nazneen Anees
    1966
    - Shaheen Currimjee
      Mauritius 1997

  - Razia Currimjee
    Mauritius 1966
    ~ Iqbal Moollan
    Mauritius 1968
    - Alexander Currimjee
      Mauritius 1990
    - Alisa Currimjee
      Mauritius 1992

- *Koser Currimjee*
  Mauritius 1938
  ~ Fakhruddin J. Currimjee
  1936

  - Arif Currimjee
    Mauritius 1962
    ~ Barbara Garbe
    Frankfurt 1963
    - Naim Currimjee
      Mauritius 1998
    - Isaak Currimjee
      Mauritius 1995

  - Azim Currimjee
    Mauritius 1964
    ~ Sarah Rawat
    Mauritius 1968
    - Karim Currimjee
      Mauritius 1996
    - Samir Currimjee
      Mauritius 1999

  - *Shenaz Currimjee*
    Mauritius 1971
    ~ Daniel de Robillard
    Mauritius 1959
    - Zakir Currimjee
      Mauritius 2002

- Abbas Currimjee
  Madagascar 1941
  ~ Geeta Biesnauthsing
  Mauritius 1946

  - Riaz Currimjee
    Mauritius 1972
  - *Maya Currimjee*
    Mauritius 1974
    ~ Ezra Jhuboo
    Dublin, Ireland 1974

- Bashirally Currimjee
  Madagascar 1943
  ~ Najma Bilgrami
  Hyderabad 1948 Deccan

  - Saeed Currimjee
    Mauritius 1977
  - Rishaad Currimjee
    Mauritius 1979

- *Farida Currimjee*
  Madagascar 1946
  ~ Michael D' Andrea
  1953 Rhode Island

Rubab Karimjee
R Zanzibar 1913 - 1994 London
~ Akber T. E. Jivanjee
Zanzibar 1912 - 1981 Mombasa

- Muzaffer Jivanjee
  Zanzibar 1935
  ~ Inge Schlier
  Germany 1939

  - *Mona Jivanjee*
    Germany 1967
    ~ Robert Carlisle
    USA 1972
    - Christopher Carlisle
      Germany 2000

  - *Noreen Jivanjee*
    Germany 1966

- *Kulsum Jivanjee*
  Dar es Salaam 1940
  ~ Abid Marvi
  Karachi 1939 - 1990 Karachi

  - Junaid Marvi
    Karachi 1965
    ~ Shahla Siddiqui
    Karachi 1970

  - *Kamila Marvi*
    Mombasa 1967
    ~ Mustafa Tapal
    Karachi 1976
    - Faazil Tapal
      Karachi 1997
    - *Bishma Tapal*
      Karachi 1999

- *Zohra Jivanjee*
  Zanzibar 1946
  ~ Zaffer Raniwala
  Korogwe 1943

  - Asif Raniwala
    London 1973
    ~ Moonira Goolamhusein
    Dubai 1977
  - *Fazila Raniwala*
    London 1977

- *Rosemine Jivanjee*
  Zanzibar 1955

CONTINUE PAGE 45

43

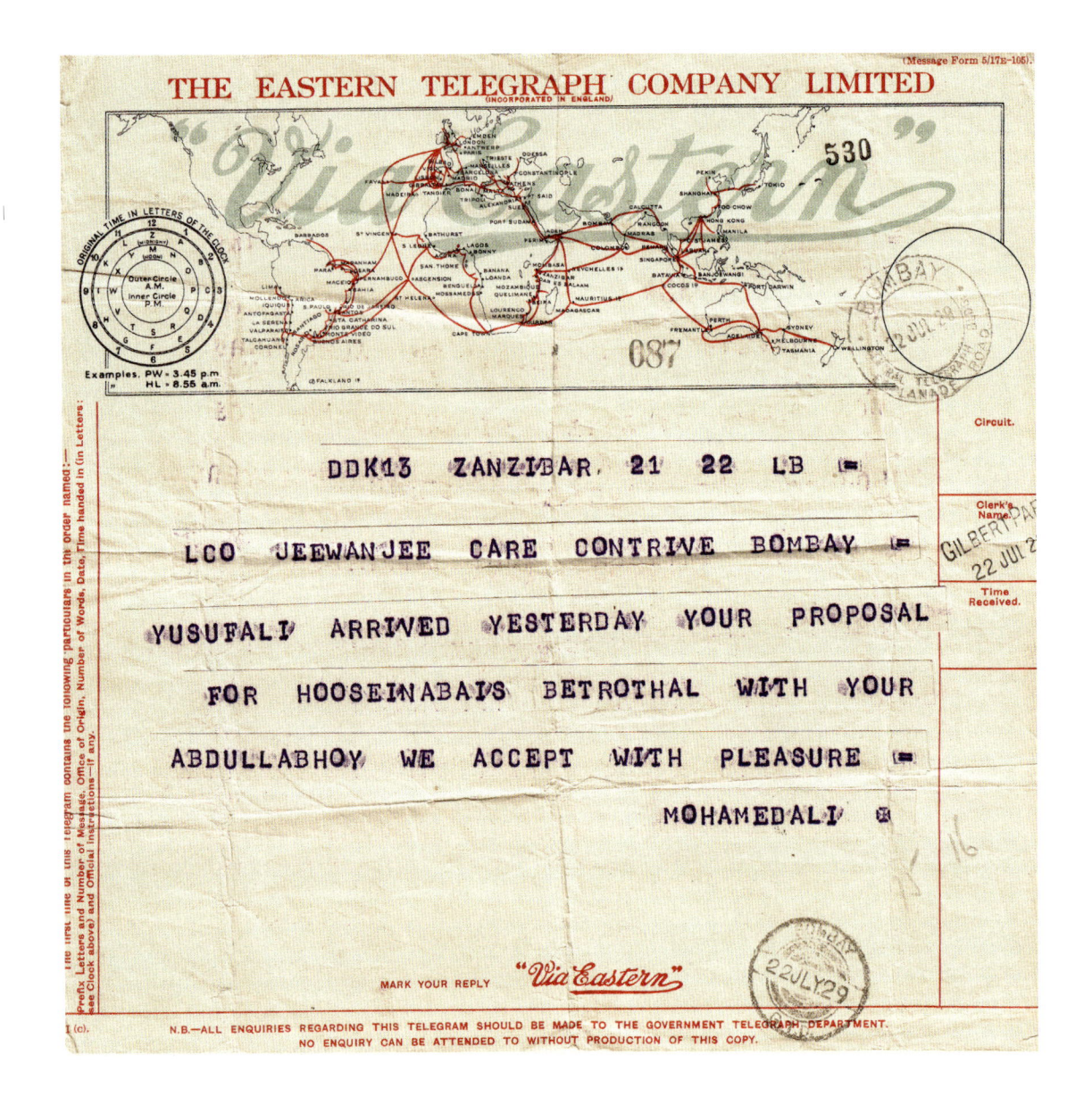

CHAPTER 3 · THE MAKING OF A TRADING EMPIRE, 1880 - 1924

The acceptance of the marrriage proposal of Huseina Karimjee and Abdulla Currimjee, dated 22 July 1929. In 1930 a 'double marriage' was organized in Zanzibar. Husseina and Abdulla married there on the same day as Abdulkarim Karimjee and Batul Noorbhai.

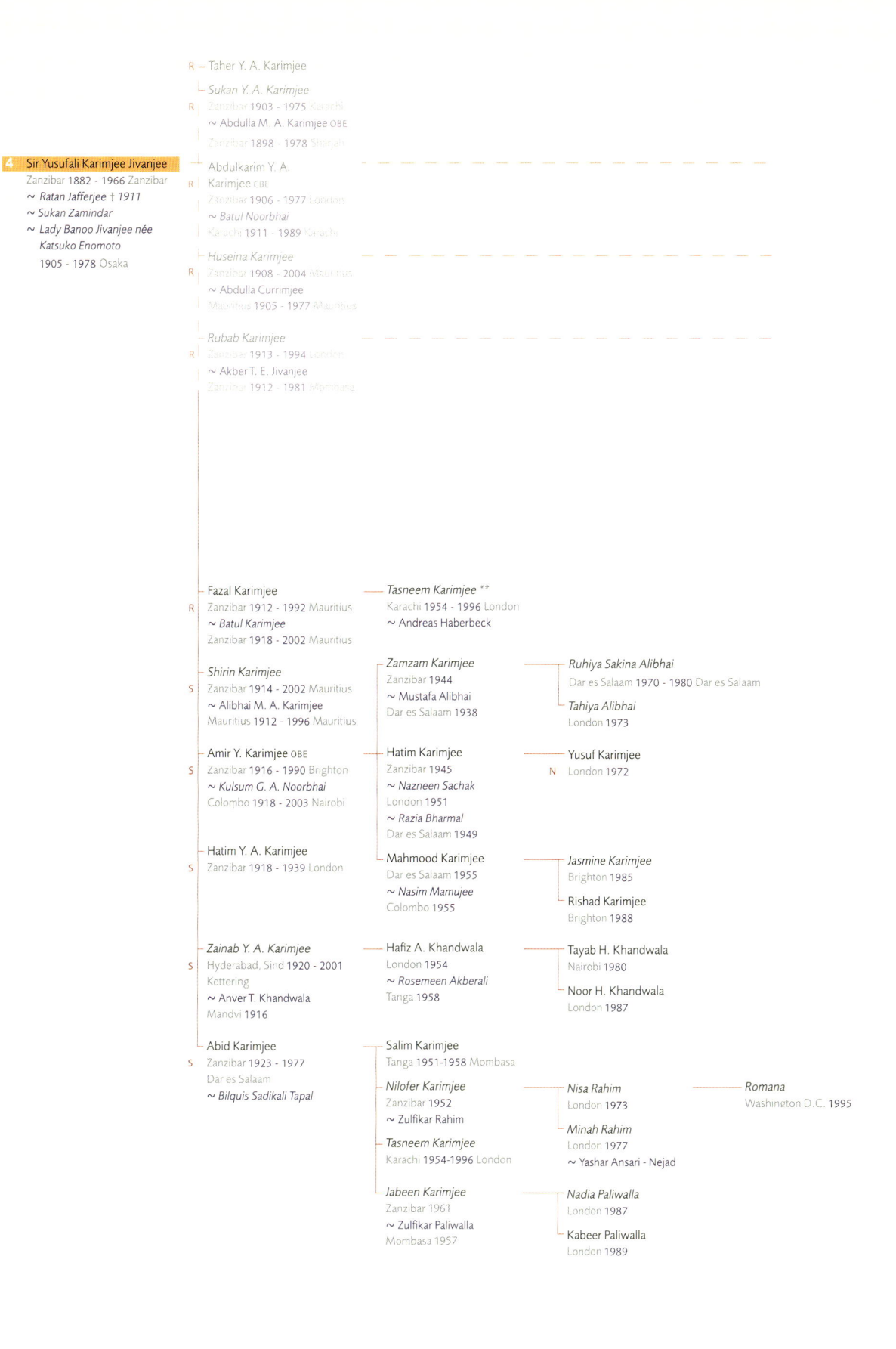

4 Sir Yusufali Karimjee Jivanjee
Zanzibar 1882 - 1966 Zanzibar
~ Ratan Jafferjee † 1911
~ Sukan Zamindar
~ Lady Banoo Jivanjee née
  Katsuko Enomoto
  1905 - 1978 Osaka

R — Taher Y. A. Karimjee
└ Sukan Y. A. Karimjee
  R Zanzibar 1903 - 1975 Karachi
     ~ Abdulla M. A. Karimjee OBE
       Zanzibar 1898 - 1978 Shirgan

  — Abdulkarim Y. A.
  R Karimjee CBE
     Zanzibar 1906 - 1977 London
     ~ Batul Noorbhai
       Karachi 1911 - 1989 Karachi

  — Huseina Karimjee
  R Zanzibar 1908 - 2004 Mauritius
     ~ Abdulla Currimjee
       Mauritius 1905 - 1977 Mauritius

  — Rubab Karimjee
  R Zanzibar 1913 - 1994 London
     ~ Akber T. E. Jivanjee
       Zanzibar 1912 - 1981 Mombasa

  — Fazal Karimjee
  R Zanzibar 1912 - 1992 Mauritius
     ~ Batul Karimjee
       Zanzibar 1918 - 2002 Mauritius

  — Shirin Karimjee
  S Zanzibar 1914 - 2002 Mauritius
     ~ Alibhai M. A. Karimjee
       Mauritius 1912 - 1996 Mauritius

  — Amir Y. Karimjee OBE
  S Zanzibar 1916 - 1990 Brighton
     ~ Kulsum G. A. Noorbhai
       Colombo 1918 - 2003 Nairobi

  — Hatim Y. A. Karimjee
  S Zanzibar 1918 - 1939 London

  — Zainab Y. A. Karimjee
  S Hyderabad, Sind 1920 - 2001
     Kettering
     ~ Anver T. Khandwala
       Mandvi 1916

  └ Abid Karimjee
  S Zanzibar 1923 - 1977
     Dar es Salaam
     ~ Bilquis Sadikali Tapal

— Tasneem Karimjee **
  Karachi 1954 - 1996 London
  ~ Andreas Haberbeck

— Zamzam Karimjee
  Zanzibar 1944
  ~ Mustafa Alibhai
    Dar es Salaam 1938

— Hatim Karimjee
  Zanzibar 1945
  ~ Nazneen Sachak
    London 1951
  ~ Razia Bharmal
    Dar es Salaam 1949

— Mahmood Karimjee
  Dar es Salaam 1955
  ~ Nasim Mamujee
    Colombo 1955

— Hafiz A. Khandwala
  London 1954
  ~ Rosemeen Akberali
    Tanga 1958

— Salim Karimjee
  Tanga 1951-1958 Mombasa

— Nilofer Karimjee
  Zanzibar 1952
  ~ Zulfikar Rahim

— Tasneem Karimjee
  Karachi 1954-1996 London

— Jabeen Karimjee
  Zanzibar 1961
  ~ Zulfikar Paliwalla
    Mombasa 1957

— Ruhiya Sakina Alibhai
  Dar es Salaam 1970 - 1980 Dar es Salaam
— Tahiya Alibhai
  London 1973

— Yusuf Karimjee
  N London 1972

— Jasmine Karimjee
  Brighton 1985
— Rishad Karimjee
  Brighton 1988

— Tayab H. Khandwala
  Nairobi 1980
— Noor H. Khandwala
  London 1987

— Nisa Rahim
  London 1973
— Minah Rahim
  London 1977
  ~ Yashar Ansari - Nejad

— Nadia Paliwalla
  London 1987
— Kabeer Paliwalla
  London 1989

— Romana
  Washington D.C. 1995

A HOUSE IN ZANZIBAR

In chapter two we saw that the family operated from the Hurumzi house in Zanzibar, but in the last quarter of the 19th century they acquired the 'Bank House' in Zanzibar. This name was given to the house after it was nationalised in the Zanzibar Revolution of 1964. It then became the 'People's Bank of Zanzibar'. Before this event, this building served as the head office of Karimjee Jivanjee & Co. Mohamedali lived above the office and most of his children were born there. There is a famous picture of three Karimjees in front of the huge Swahili-style door of the 'Bank House'. The picture was taken after the agency agreement with Caltex for the distribution of oil products had been finalised in 1924. On the right we see the young Tayabali Karimjee (1897 - 1987). He had just started his career in the Karimjee family following the early death of his father in 1918. On the left we see Yusufali Karimjee (1882 - 1966) who was the born trader and 'outward bound' manager of the Karimjee businesses. In the middle we see Mohamedali Karimjee (1877 - 1940), who managed the business affairs from the head office in Zanzibar. These three names come up quite often during the course of the Karimjee Jivanjee family history. In fact, they shape the three male lines in the Karimjee family tree.

The 'Bank House' was initially known as 'the German Club' and it belonged to the German merchant Rudolph Heinrich Ruete. He worked for the famous German trading company Hansing & Co., and later married the famous Arab Princess Salme.[19] The most striking feature of this building is, of course, the Zanzibari door. These types of doors have a long history in Zanzibar, but this door remains to this day one of the most outstanding examples of craftsmanship, quality of wood and fine details.

The earliest dated 'Zanzibari door' dates back as far as 1700 (A.D.) and is a clear relic of the Indian Ocean maritime history.

It was the result of constant cultural interaction between the Arab world, South Asia and the Swahili Coast. Some doors may have been originally imported from India or Oman. Later, well-off Arab and Indian traders would hire Indian craftsmen to build a door. During the 19th century, special craftsmen in Zanzibar developed a style and tradition of carving wooden doors that can be found nowhere else in the world! Their special style combined methods and techniques from Western India with decorative elements from the Islamic and Swahili traditions. When a house was built in Zanzibar, the door was traditionally the first part to be erected: the greater the wealth and social position of the house's owner, the larger and more elaborately carved his front door was. As Richard Burton commented in 1857; "the higher the tenement, the bigger the gateway, the heavier the padlock and the huge iron studs that nail the door of heavy timber, the greater is the owner's dignity."[20] In a contemporary well-researched book, this door is referred to as the 'Mona Lisa of the Zanzibari doors.' It is said to have been duplicated more than ten times, but its intricacy and the quality of timber could never be matched.[21]

The Karimjee Zanzibar office was nationalised after the Zanzibar Revolution of 1964, after which it became the People's Bank of Zanzibar. The Karimjee door was featured on Tanzanian banknotes in the 1990s.

Two brothers and a nephew in 1924. From right to left: Yusufali Karimjee, Mohamedali Karimjee and Tayabali Karimjee. This was the front door of the Karimjee office in Zanzibar. Note that the two squares at the top were specially made for the Karimjees. Normally, the round line would be unbroken.

CHAPTER 3 · THE MAKING OF A TRADING EMPIRE, 1880 - 1924

PORTRAIT

YUSUFALI KARIMJEE 1882 - 1966

The life of Yusufali Karimjee is characterised by unexpected moves, adventures, and hard work. However, most striking was his great entrepreneurial spirit. He was bold enough to overcome racial barriers in his business life as well as his personal life. His life raises interesting questions like: why did he marry a Japanese woman? What was he doing in Germany just before the outbreak of the Second World War? What were the secrets of his success? Some of his stories are still partly shrouded in mystery because little is known about his life. But what is known, however, is surprising and so exceptional that it reads like an adventure story. In order to understand some of these stories, we have to go back in time and realise that people rarely travelled by steamer, flying was not yet possible, and there were no air conditioning systems in East Africa until the 1950s.

Yusufali Karimjee was born in 1882 in Zanzibar and spent much of his early life on the island. He joined the Karimjee family business with his older brothers Hassanali and Mohamedali in 1895 at the age of 13. He soon realised two important facts of life. One was that in order to defend the business interests of South Asians in East Africa they would need to organise themselves. That is why he became President of the Indian Merchant Association in East Africa in the first decade of the 20th century. Second, at an early age he was very aware that the world was bigger than just Zanzibar. He made his first trip to England and Europe in 1910 as part of an Asian delegation headed by A.M Jeevanjee (not related) from Nairobi. They went to London to publicise Indian grievances related to discriminatory legislation, and to appeal to the more humanitarian and liberal elements of British Society (see picture page 130).

He married three times. His first wife Ratan gave birth to six children. His first child Taher died at an early age. After this tragic event, Ratan gave birth to five healthy children, Sukan, Abdulkarim, Husseina, Rubab and Fazal. Unfortunately Ratan died in 1911 and he therefore got married a second time to a Bohra woman called Sukan Zamindar. She gave birth to five children, Shirin, Amir, Hatim, Zainab and Abid. However, unfortunately, she also died early, although we don't know exactly when. He then married a woman whom he had met during his numerous travels to Japan: Katsuko Enomoto. He had no children with his third wife.

An African Asian married to a Japanese woman would today be considered an unconventional combination. But in the 1930s this was a multi-cultural combination avant la lettre. Very little is known about how they met and why, and how he proposed to her. Moreover, we have little clue as to how people in Japan, Africa or Europe responded to the presence of Yusufali and Katusko in their midst. One story, which has not been confirmed, reveals that he met her on one of his trips to Japan. He had caught a cold or flu on the ship and went to a private clinic upon arriving in Osaka. He met her and fell in love with his nurse. She came from a very noble family as she went to the same school as the aunt of Mr Toyoda (Toyota). They probably married before the Second World War but Yusufali decided to bring her to Dar es Salaam in the early 1950's only, where she was affectionately known as 'Okasan' (mother).

Yusufali Karimjee travelled a lot to the East. He mainly

Yusufali Karimjee dressed in Bohra turban and long sleeves around 1910.

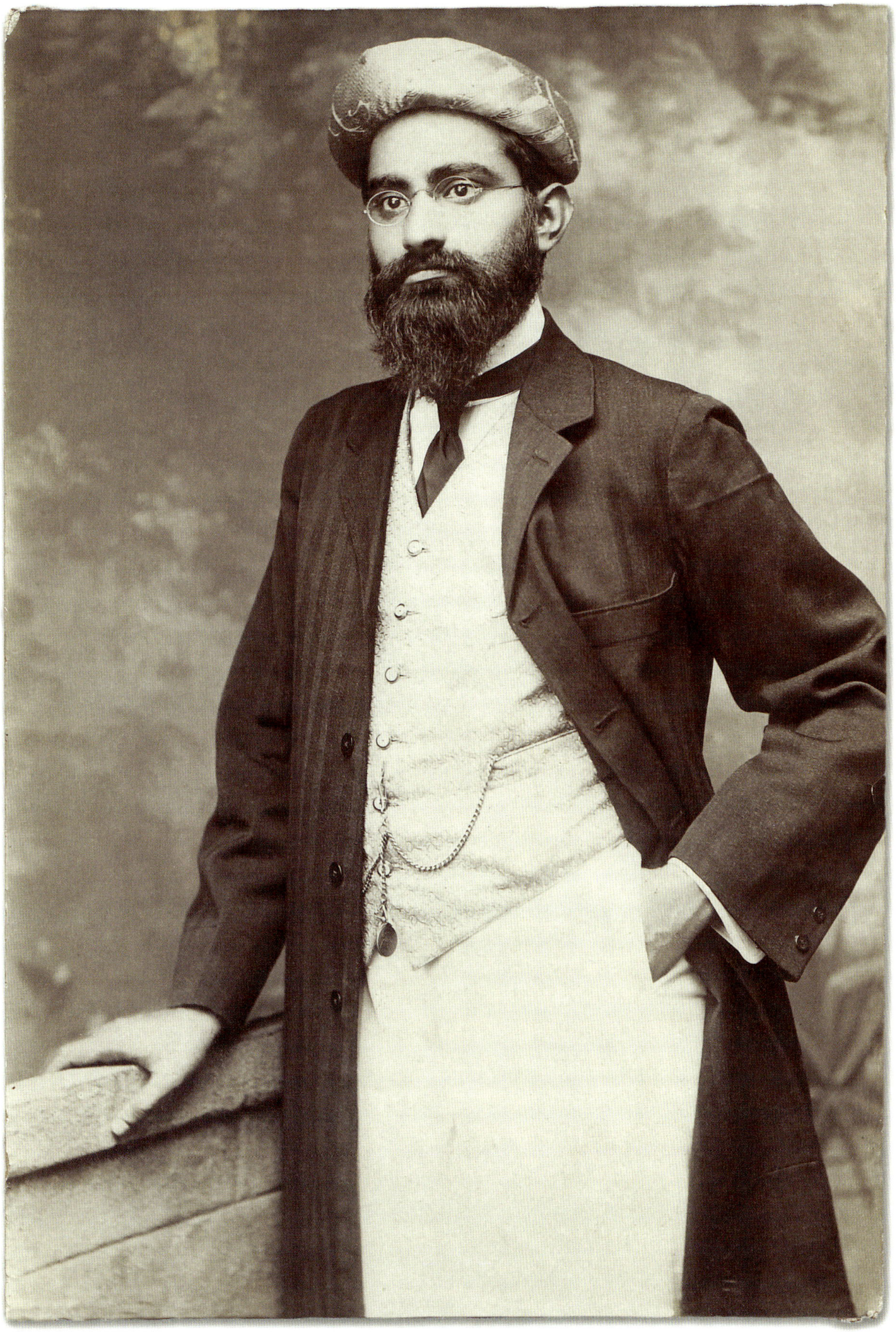

travelled by steamer, which was very unusual for someone from the Indian subcontinent. Most of his fellow-passengers would have been Europeans at that time. His favourite destinations included Zanzibar, Karachi, Bombay, Colombo, Rangoon, Singapore, Bangkok, Hong Kong and Kobe in Japan. In all these places he would visit Bohra friends. In Colombo he was close to the Akberallys, Noorbhais and the Esufallys. In Mauritius, Yusufali was close to the Currimjees, the Kakals and the Ismails. In Bangkok, Yusufali would definitely see the Maskati family, whereas in Honk Kong, Kobe and Osaka (Japan) he would visit the Barma family who had relatives there. The Karimjee family eventually would marry into some of these families. The Currimjees of Mauritius are still closely related through marriage.

Upon his arrival on foreign shores, Yusufali would be primarily concerned with two major issues. One was the European food on the ship since Indian food was not served on the steamers. Therefore, whenever he disembarked from the ship he would say: "I am not talking to anyone, until I have rice and dhal. I have been eating this European food for weeks now." A second issue was his intense interest in the prices of almost every product available in the market. While the trade with the East and the Far East was prosperous, Yusufali explored new markets in Europe as well.

Yusufali continued to perform his political duties as well. He was one of the delegates to the Secretary of State in 1923 representing the Tanganyika Indian community. This was, again, in connection with legislation that was not favourable for the Indian business community. In this capacity he earned himself the nickname of the 'Lion of Zanzibar'.[22] This nickname conjures up the image of the strong, bold independent personality that he was. He received considerably rewards from the local rulers for his services to the community, for example, the Sultan of Zanzibar honoured him with the Brilliant Star of Zanzibar. In addition, in 1912 the Sultan of Turkey honoured him with the Star of Majidivah for his contributions to the Red Crescent work during the Tripolitanian War (1911 - 1912).

In 1929, he was involved in a bad accident while sailing from Mikindani (in southern Tanganyika) on the Holland Line ship Ystroom to Zanzibar. On 27 June he went for an after-dinner walk on deck. A Chinese worker in the bunker room had left a manhole open to get ventilation below even though this was strictly forbidden. It was dark and Yusufali was reciting his prayers when he fell 17 feet down into the hold. He lost consciousness and had suffered serious injuries and was bleeding profusely. The ship had no doctor and so it was diverted to Dar es Salaam. He had suffered serious injuries to the head and body and had a fractured jaw and was bruised all over. He spent three weeks in Dar es Salaam and then returned home to Zanzibar in a wheel chair. He was able to walk a little after six weeks. The doctors advised him to rest, cease all business responsibilities, and go away to a cooler climate. He decided to sail by the German Africa Line ship Usambara to Germany for rest and treatment. He was advised that if he wanted to recover quickly he should avoid living in hot and humid countries.

Yusufali spent a few years in Japan, Hong Kong and Britain, but still paid regular visits to Tanganyika and Zanzibar during the cool seasons. It seems plausible, however, that he continued to travel a lot. His passport issued on 19 January 1935 has numerous stamps from countries in Europe and South- and South-East Asia. In the late 1930s he most probably lived in Japan for a while. In 1938, he sent a set of pictures taken by a professional photographer of his house in Uozaki in Japan to his sons in East Africa. Uozaki is a waterfront suburb of Kobe.

Karimjee Jivanjee & Co. informed it's business associates – in this case the German East Africa Line – that Yusufali was unable to fulfil his obligations due to an accident. The letter is dated 17th August 1929.

ESTABLISHED 1825.

BRANCHES:
MOMBASA, DAR-ES-SALAAM, TANGA AND LINDI.

KARIMJEE JIVANJEE & Co.

TELEGRAPHIC ADDRESS:
"KARIMJEE"

A. B. C. 5TH & 6TH EDITIONS
A I
LIEBERS
BENTLEYS
PRIVATES
} CODES USED

P. O. Box 91.

ZANZIBAR, ... 19......

(17th August 1929)

THE CIRCULAR LETTER.

Our Mr. Yusufali A. K. Jivanjee had a serious accident on board the steamer on 27th June last, while returning from his usual trip of inspection of our plantations in the Tanganyika Territory and although he has now greatly improved, it has been found necessary to take a trip to Europe for further treatment, if that would be found necessary and for change of climate.

He is therefore sailing today per s. s. "Usambara" for Genoa and will thence proceed to Germany. He is accompanied by Mrs. Jivanjee and his son Mr. Abdulkarim Y. A. K. Jivanjee.

It is uncertain whether he will be able in this trip to pay you a visit. But even then he will try his best to do so.

If it is found necessary to communicate with him, his present address is as under:—

Yusufali A. K. Jivanjee
c/o The Deutsche-Ost-Afrika Linie,
Afrikahaus,
HAMBURG.

Yours faithfully,

KARIMJEE JIVANJEE & Co.

The pictures show a European-style house. Most of the furniture is also in European style. Some artefacts on the tables and the floor have a more oriental design and there is also a leopard's skin from East Africa. The pictures describe the house as 'Uozaki residence'. One picture shows the beautifully designed garden with the then 56-year-old Yusufali looking straight and proud into the camera. Some pictures are signed as 'father' others are signed as Yusufali A.K. Jivanjee. Interestingly enough, the pictures do not show his Japanese wife. Maybe he did not want to offend his children with a picture of her? Maybe he was not married to her yet? The letters include questions relating to the well-being of his children, suggestions about marriage proposals and some passages on business issues.

Because of his extensive travels, Yusufali Karimjee's passport is covered in stamps. His British passport raises some interesting questions about the importance and extent of his trading business. He went to Hamburg on 10 May 1939. The German invasion of Poland in September of that year marked the start of the Second World War. The stamps show that he left Germany on 29 May only a few months before the war started. Remember that Yusufali was a British subject with dark Asian skin. His European dress and attitude would certainly not have been sufficient reason to convince the Nazis of his status and background. A trip to Germany must have been very unpleasant. His passport also shows that he withdrew a considerable amount of money from the Dresdener Bank in Bad Neuheim (Germany). Was he finalising some important business transaction, sensing that Europe would be entering a war soon? Or was there some other reason?

It so happened that the Karimjees had an important agent in Hamburg, by the name of Johannes Koch, known as 'Hanni' among the Karimjees. Hanni Koch was a commodity trader and was a prominent buyer of sisal from Tanganyika. During the war he was in charge of the supplies division responsible for buying

Ichiyo Studio

*Uozaki Residence
Japan
15th/4 March 1938*

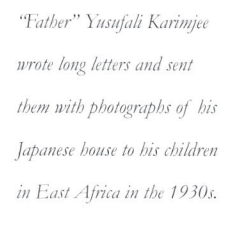

"Father" Yusufali Karimjee wrote long letters and sent them with photographs of his Japanese house to his children in East Africa in the 1930s.

essential commodities such as sugar, tea, sisal and kapok, etc. While Yusufali was in Hamburg, he was staying in the prestigious Hotel Die Vier Jahreszeiten (The Four Seasons). During this visit the German army commandeered the hotel for housing the military unit and Yusufali was promptly requested to vacate it.

Hanni Koch, quickly intervened and was able to remind the German commandant that Indians were Aryans, and therefore Yusufali was allowed to stay in the hotel for a few more weeks until his departure, although he wasn't to leave Germany yet.

The passport of Yusufali Karimjee showing his date of

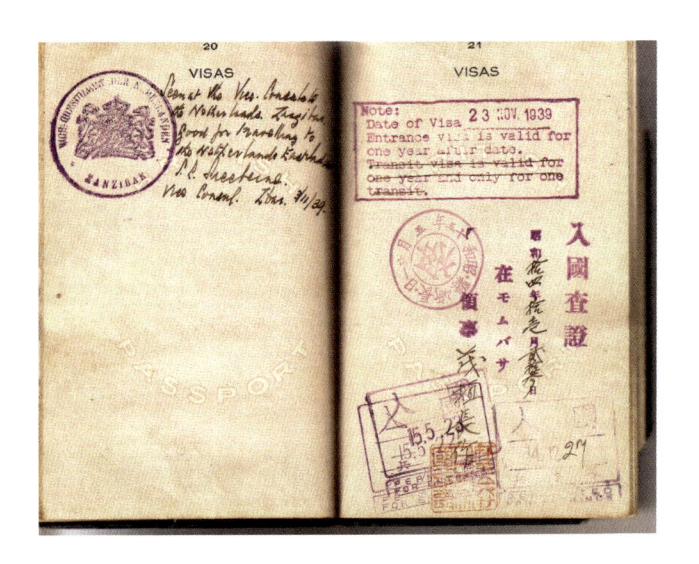

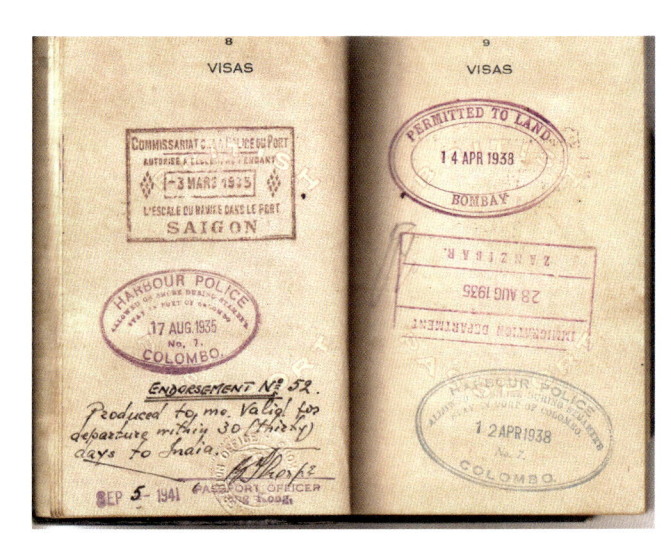

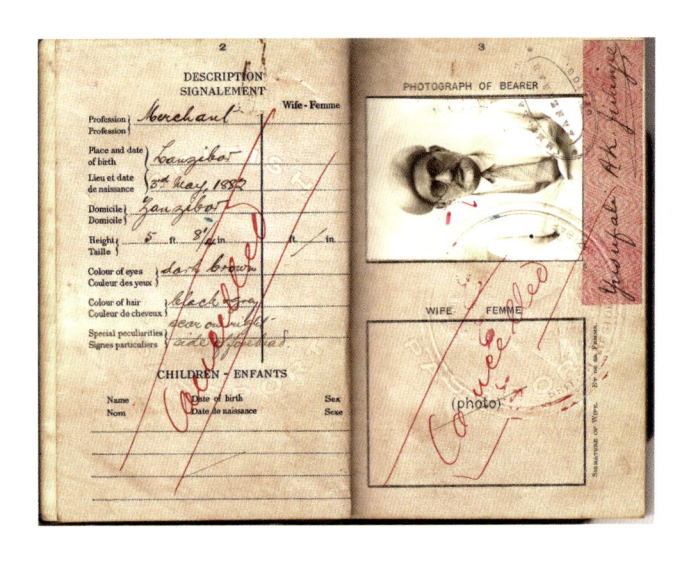

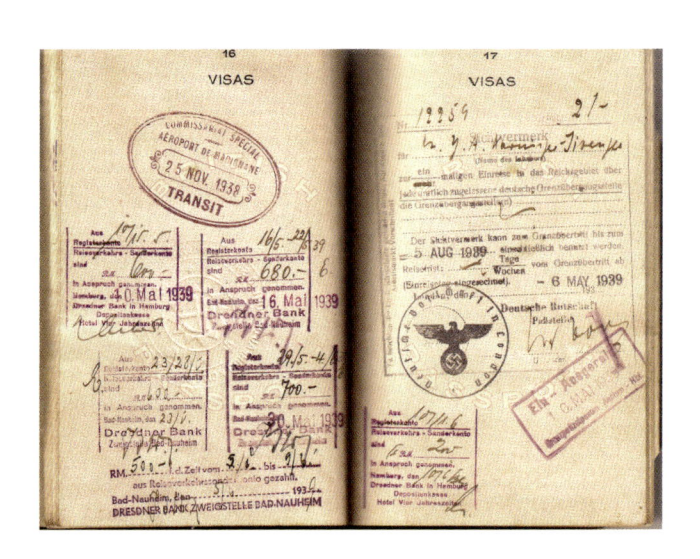

An old passport of Yususfali Karimjee, showing his extensive travels.

CHAPTER 3 · THE MAKING OF A TRADING EMPIRE, 1880 - 1924

The houseboat in Kashmir called 'The Star of Zanzibar'. Pictures probably taken in the Second World War.

birth (3 May 1882) and profession (note that, modestly, 'trader' has been used). The passport is filled with various immigrations stamps, showing his extensive travels, including to Germany in May 1939.

Bad Neuheim was a popular health resort specialising in heart and lung diseases. It was home to the William G. Kerckhoff Institute, which was one of the most important centres for heart research at that time. The letter that announced the Yusafali's accident on board a steamer in the Zanzibar harbour in 1929, states that he went to Germany, probably for a medical check-up. Again, we can't be certain but it seems plausible that Yusufali went to Bad Neuheim to see his doctors. He must have been aware that this was possibly his last chance to do so.[23] Nevertheless, it is equally possible that his German business associates advised him to visit Bad Neuheim as a place where many upper class people would enjoy their leisure time in those days.

After the trip to Germany, he went to Hong Kong in November 1939 and to India in September 1940. By then, India, as a part of the British Empire, was at war with Germany. Yusufali realised that one of his sons, Amir, was still in the UK where he was studying. Amir – being a British subject – wanted to join the Royal Air Force. Yusufali was convinced that the Karimjees should not join the 'white men's war'. Yusufali ordered his son to come to India where they owned a houseboat (called 'The Star of Zanzibar') in Kashmir. He did not know that his order for his son to return to India would result in his son having the adventure of his life. The Tanganyika Herald of April 17th 1969 relates:

"One cold morning he (Amir) set sail from Liverpool in a cargo passenger vessel and on the high seas joined a large convoy. It took a month to reach Cape Town, but that month, he said, seemed like an eternity. The convoy had not been underway for very long before the first U-boat was sighted. Ships were being blown up day and night and Mr Amir saw at least five ships near his ship go down in flames. The most frightening experience of the whole voyage was when he and many others on board watched a German torpedo miss his vessel by about three yards." [24]

Interestingly, it was at the houseboat in Kashmir that Amir first met his future wife Kulsum Noorbhai. It was not until 1953 that Yusufali settled in Dar es Salaam permanently. His intense desire to be near his children and grandchildren in his old age could be fulfilled, thanks to the invention of air conditioning. This invention enabled him to survive the hot and humid climate of Dar es Salaam. By then he had retired and enjoyed his role as the senior family member.

He bought a house near Ocean Rd., which at that time was situated in an area where only whites lived. Consequently, the house was bought through a European lawyer. Many of his grandchildren remember him as a very formal, strict and distinguished man. Most of them were expected to visit him at least once a day and often this was a very formal and tense moment for them.

Sir Yusufali Karimjee and Lady Banoo Jivanjee in London after Yusufali had been knighted in 1958. Yusufali's son Amir and his wife Kulsum accompanied them.

In 1958, he was knighted by the Queen, a distinction which was the crowning glory of his life's work. His motto: 'Work, save and give' and 'Wealth imposes obligations' were finally recognised by the Empire. He set up several charities and was known as one of the foremost philanthropists in Tanganyika (see chapter six).

Yusufali died in 1966, leaving his Japanese wife, then called Lady Banoo Jivanjee, eight surviving children and numerous grandchildren. He was buried in Dar es Salaam. After the death of Yusufali, his Japanese wife Okasan (Lady Banoo Jivanjee) went to live in Brighton, UK with Amir. After a year, she returned to Japan where she retired in a modest house in Osaka. One family member was designated to look after her and visit her every year. In addition, the Bohra friends in Japan (the Barmas) looked after her until she died in Osaka in 1978, where she was buried in the Muslim section of the foreigners' cemetery high on a hill overlooking Osaka harbour. Even today some family members still make the long trip to visit Okasan's burial place.

YUSUFALI KARIMJEE

1882	Born in Zanzibar
1895	Joins the family business
1900 - 1920	Marries twice and has eleven children, engages in trade with South and East Asia
1910	First visit to Europe
1912	Sultan of Turkey honours him with the Star of Majidivah
1920	Joins South Asian business interest organisations
1929	Suffers accident on ship
1930s	Lives in Japan
1935	Passport filled with travel stamps
1939	Travels to Germany
1940 - 45	Travels throughout South and East Asia
1948	Visits Mauritius
1953	Retires in Dar es Salaam with Lady Banoo Jivanjee
1955	Opening of Karimjee Hall in Dar es Salaam (see page 134)
1958	Honoured with knighthood
1966	Dies, is buried in Dar es Salaam

Yusufali Karimjee was buried in the Dawoodi Bohra cemetery in Dar es Salaam in 1966.

The tombstone of Lady Banoo Yusufali in the Muslim section of the graveyard in Osaka. She was buried according to Muslim tradition in 1978.

CHAPTER 4

From trades to estates

1925 - 1963

The classical western developmental pattern from trade to industry was not an option for entrepreneurs and businessmen in East Africa. It was clear to most merchants that the conditions for industrialisation in Africa were poor. The other option to diversify the trading business into a 'producing' business was to invest in agriculture. Therefore, the Karimjee family decided to spread their interests from trades to estates when the opportunity arose. Consequently, they started to diversify and do business in coffee, tea and sisal plantations. Sisal would become one of the major money-spinners for the family in the period just after the Second World War. In addition they set up a separate business unit under the name International Motor Mart, which became the agents for Nash Cars, Francis-Barnett Motor Cycles, and Rootes Group. Last but not least, the Karimjees started the 'properties' division, to manage the growing number of offices, stores and other buildings the company owned.

A new era of political and economic stability was emerging after the First World War. German East Africa had come under British military rule and its transfer to Britain under the 1919 Treaty of Versailles was confirmed by a League of Nations mandate in 1922. It was later to become a United Nations Trust Territory, with Britain changing the name to 'Tanganyika Territory'. The inland market was extended through the addition of British East Africa, known today as Kenya and Uganda. Moreover, India was still part of the British Empire. Therefore, in much of the area similar economic regulations, licences and tax systems applied. The economy of the Indian Ocean region appeared prosperous and the European interest in the African region was growing. European planters and settlers, as well as the colonial government, were investing in the African economy.

This was the time for new investment and diversification. One of the major new prospects was the option to buy 'Enemy Properties', i.e. land and buildings that formerly belonged to Germans before the war. But seeing new potential was not

MAP 3 **POLITICAL MAP OF EAST AFRICA**

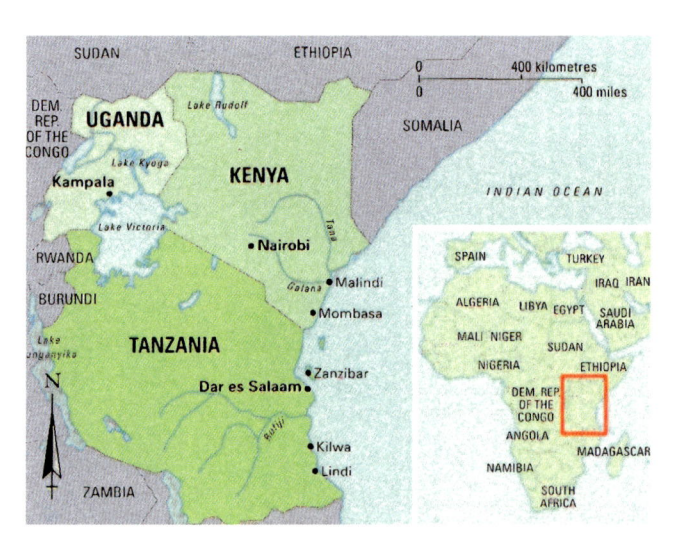

Source: Brij Lal (ed), *The Encyclopedia of the Indian Diaspora,* Singapore 2006, p. 255.

enough to create new wealth. It was soon evident that the Indians were being excluded from the auctions where the properties were being sold. This is just one of the examples that demonstrate how colonial society was organised along racial lines. Everyone was treated equally, but whites were treated more equally. Not everyone had the same economic opportunities. Nevertheless – as we have seen in the first chapters – Asians were more than able to organise themselves. The Indian Government including the Viceroy successfully petitioned for Indians to receive the same treatment as other British subjects. The Tanganyika colonial government eventually allowed Indians to participate in bidding.

Around the same time, Yusufali was taking his usual afternoon walk in Dar es Salaam. It is said that he had had a long chat with a Greek plantation owner. The Greek suggested that he should buy some land and start his own plantation. Initially, Yusufali was not interested. The Karimjees were doing well and owning land could get them into trouble, because it is often difficult to sell off land quickly. In addition, they didn't have any experience with land ownership, nor with running plantations.

To him it seemed to be a long-term investment with a low rate of return. But the Greek was able to convince him that good money was to be made with plantations and the initial investments would pay for themselves within five or six years after the plantations started to produce. In other words, money was to be made: Yusufali was interested. He eventually guided the family into the estate business, as he bought the landed properties after the First World War.

The schedules of properties offered for sale were published in the Tanga Post and East Coast Advertiser and the London Times. At the first sale in May 1921, Indians bought at least 15 of the 40 business lots auctioned in Dar es Salaam. The total amount invested by Indians was more than 50,000 pounds sterling of a total of 112,000 pounds sterling.[25] Of the Indian bidders, Yusufali Karimjee was the most active, buying a whole range of real estate and land. The Tanga Post and East Coast Advertiser of 11 June 1920 mentions 20 lots, 15 of which were bought by the Karimjees. This included: (1) a sisal and rubber plantation of 292 hectares, situated near Ruvu on the Central Railway (Dar es Salaam, 6,250 pounds sterling); (2) a plot of

Article related to the disposal of enemy property, Tanga Post, 11th December 1922.

> **SATURDAY APRIL 1st, 1922**　　DAR-ES-SALAAM TIMES
>
> ## TANGANYIKA TERRITORY.
> ### DISPOSAL OF ENEMY PROPERTY.
>
> Pursuant to the conditions of the Enemy Property (Disposal) Proclamation 1920 and in accordance with Section 3 (2) thereof notice is hereby give it is proposed to expose for sale by public auction at Dar-es-Salaam on Monday the 3rd day of July, 1922 at 10 a. m. as per term of Section 3 (1) of th Proclamation the respective rights titles and interests specified in the third column of the schedule hereto in the immovable properties described in the column of the said schedule.
>
> The particulars given in this schedule are liable to alteration and any property may be withdrawn without notice.
>
> Copies of the conditions of sale may be obtained from Mr W. J. Moynagh, Auctioneer, Dar-es-Salaam, (and Nairobi) Mr. L. Gordon Sandford, Empire Piccadilly W. 1, or the undersigned.
>
> **ERNEST ADAMS**
> *Custodian of Enemy Property.*
>
> DAR-ES-SALAAM,
> TANGANYIKA TERRITORY,
> Monday, July 3rd. 1922

A notification of enemy properties in local newspapers: Dar es Salaam Times, Saturday 1 April 1922.

land of 41 ar. 34 sq.m., together with a three-storey building of offices and living quarters, a two-storey building being used as living quarters and printing works, as well as a range of stabling stores, garages, etc. (all in Dar es Salaam for a total of 8,500 pounds sterling); and (3) a coconut plantation of 50 hectares, situated on the old Bagamoyo Road (650 pounds sterling). The investments totalled more than 38,000 pounds sterling.[26]

The property market and agricultural business, in everything from tea and coffee plantations to kapok estates and sisal plantations, were a novel departure for Karimjee Jivanjee Co. Ltd, from its usual objects. The process of managing capital and labour in a trading company differs significantly from that of enterprise in agricultural production. In a trading company, the balance between buying and selling goods generates the profits. However, throughout the agricultural production of goods a range of constantly changing factors affect the profit margins. These include the price of seeds and raw material, the price of labour, the price of machines, and changes in government legislation regarding labour, the environment, taxes and the efficiency of management. Moreover, 'estates' do not 'just sit there'. The process of cutting trees, developing land, working with seeds and fertilisers, training a labour force, and many other things had to be developed. In the Karimjee Jivanjee family, it was Abdulla Mohamedali Karimjee who became the prime entrepreneur, manager and foreman of the estate business.

By 1924, the firm had acquired six sisal estates, and eventually became the third largest sisal producer in the world. The extensive nature of the plantation work of Karimjee Jivanjee Estates Ltd. can be measured based on the fact that it employed a large army of labourers, numbering between 12,000 and 15,000. It also employed 40 European managers, assistants and engineers who were English, Germans, Greek, Italian, Dutch, Swiss, Indian and Sri Lankan nationals.[27] The bookkeepers and clerks were generally Indians.[28]

The Karimjees (and other plantation owners as well) realised that part of the success of the plantation business depended on their relations with workers. The training and the control of workers formed one of the major challenges in the estate

CHAPTER 4 · FROM TRADES TO ESTATES 1925 - 1963

The type of labour lines rapidly disappearing from sisal estates. Image from the 1950s.

New permanent houses, typical of those many sisal estates were building. A Karimjee sisal estate around 1952.

business. The Karimjee Jivanjee Estates Ltd. is said to have been 'probably the first in the whole of East Africa in the care it takes and the solicitude it shows in the maintenance and welfare of its large numbers of labourers. (…) On its Soga plantation, the firm has erected a mosque for labourers and its dispensary for them. On the Gomba plantation (….) a special hospital has been provided with a European nurse in charge. On the Kidugalo Estate also, a hospital has been built and efforts are being made to provide every one of its plantations with such a hospital.'[29] This evidence clearly shows that the relations with labourers were highly valued.

In addition to the diversification to the estate development, a second phase of diversification was the expansion of the car, car parts, and petroleum business. This all started with a trading license to sell kerosene. The American-owned The Texas Co. started to export oil to South Africa in 1908. Three years later, The Texas Co. formed a subsidiary based in Cape Town. The Texas Co. (South Africa) Ltd. quickly became a leader in the South African market, advertising its products effectively, building a strong marketing and distribution network, and establishing one of the nation's first filling stations in 1922.

In 1924, The Texas Company, predecessors of Caltex, decided to start exporting to Tanganyika and with this in mind, they sent their representative, Mr Boyac, to Zanzibar to find a suitable agent. To this day, one of the central images of Karimjee Jivanjee & Co. is a picture showing Mr Boyac standing in front of the original headquarters of Karimjee Jivanjee & Co. Zanzibar in the background (1924, see page 47). It had just finalised a new business deal. The Karimjees would take up the license of Caltex and sell petrol and kerosene in East Africa.

In those early years, it was said that any sale of five or more tins of kerosene or petrol was personally attended to by one of the family members, where other firms might well have left such sales to their subordinates.[30] Abdulhusein Adamjee, a cousin

CHAPTER 4 · FROM TRADES TO ESTATES 1925 – 1963

Advertising Texas Company. The Karimjees advertised their licenses in East Africa in Gujarati as well as English. This advertisement is taken from the silver jubilee issue of the paper Samarch in December 1936.

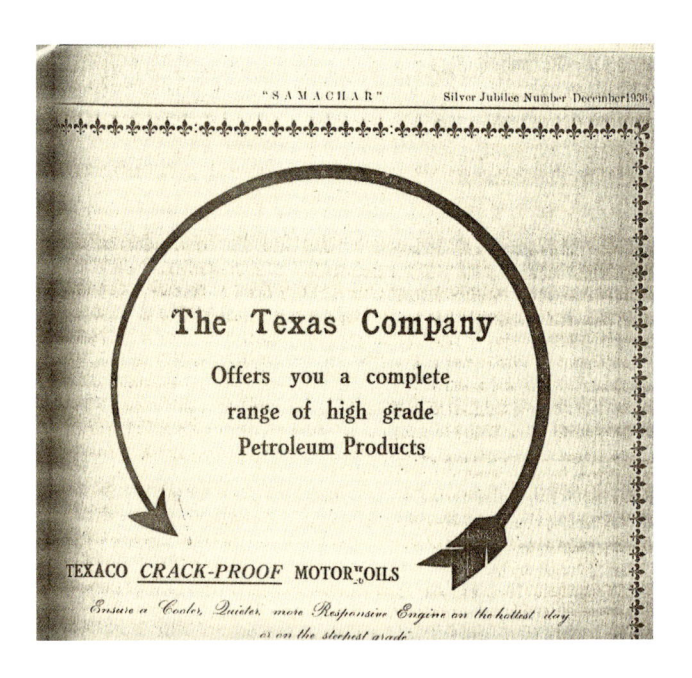

of the family, who had begun life as a departmental manager, was very much involved in the early years of the petrol sales. His extreme attention to detail, coupled with a will to please the humblest of customers was an integral part of the firm. In the early 20s Caltex products came from the United States (a giant refinery in Bahrain in the Persian Gulf was built many years later) and was brought to Zanzibar on board cargo ships. Dhows supplied Dar es Salaam with petrol, oils and kerosene, transporting two to three hundred cans at a time. In 1953, however, the sales, excluding those to the government, averaged 120,000 gallons of kerosene and 250,000 gallons of motor spirit every month. After that, Caltex set up its own branch in Tanganyika, but the Karimjees kept the agency for Tanga, the Southern Provinces and for Zanzibar.[31]

In 1927 a subsidiary was started in Tanga and Dar es Salaam under the name The International Motor Mart (IMM). The basic aim was to provide East Africa with motorbikes, cars and spare parts. It needed cars and tractors for its agricultural business and assumed that other plantation owners, as well as the small African, European and Asian elite would be interested as well. Yusufali's son Abdulkarim became the executive manager of this division (see his portrait in chapter five). Within an incredibly short time it was able to deal with the most important car and motor dealers in the world. They had no previous experience in the automotive industry or the business of spare parts. This again is evidence of the importance of keeping up a good name, because it is all one has.

IMM soon became the agent for Triumph Motors, whose motor cycles have achieved a cult status among the youth. IMM imported the well-known Nash Cars (founded in 1916 by former General Motors president Charles W. Nash, who acquired the Thomas B. Jeffery Company). It was also the agent for International Trucks and Francis-Barnett Motor Cycles (Francis-Barnett was a British motorcycle manufacturer founded in 1919,

A showroom of the International Motor Mart, Dar es Salaam. Note the 'Caltex' sign on the right.

by Gordon Francis and Arthur Barnett). IMM soon acted as an agent for the Rootes Group (originally founded in Kent in 1919 by William Rootes as a car sales company). Furthermore, IMM was the representative of International Harvester for tractors and agricultural machinery. This diversification shows a clear progression, whereby the experience in selling oil products and car parts merged with the new venture of the estates, because trucks and agricultural machines were needed. Therefore, it was only to be expected that a profitable collaboration with car companies would benefit the estate business, while also boosting the export figures of those companies.

The rapid expansion of new companies resulted in the formal separation of trading, properties and agricultural divisions. This was necessary in order to clearly identify legal ownership and management. The parent company remained Karimjee Jivanjee & Co. Ltd., whilst each company had a similar family shareholding and Board of Directors, which consisted mainly of family members. At this juncture we need to recognise the role of late Akberally Adamjee. Mr Adamjee was recruited from India in the 1930s to assist the young Karimjees in the management and administration of the business. He was a very capable administrator and became a senior manager and also the first non-family director in the business. He was mainly active in Karimjee Jivanjee & Co. Ltd, and Karimjee Properties. He had specialised in handling the Insurance and Shipping agencies. Akber Adamjee received an OBE (Officer of the British Empire) from the Queen in the 1950s. His nephew Hakim Adamjee later married Fizza, the daughter of Sir Tayabali Karimjee (see the portrait of Sir Tayabali, page 138).

There is no doubt that the diversification benefited from the vertical and horizontal integration within the Karimjee group of companies. For example Karimjee Jivanjee Estates' agricultural activities benefited from the auto and agro agencies of IMM, as well as the tyre agency. Karimjee Jivanjee Estates would take advantage of the insurance and shipping services of Karimjee Jivanjee & Co. Ltd. as well as the Caltex agencies. Tea and sisal would be exported and the Clearing & Forwarding section of the shipping division of Karimjee Jivanjee & Co. Ltd. would import machinery parts.

Abdulla Karimjee played a prominent role in the Tanzanian Sisal Marketing Association (TASMA) in Tanga.

In summary, after World War I, the trading company Karimjee Jivanjee & Co. Ltd. diversified in various directions. Most importantly, the Karimjees went into the estate business, with the sisal estates proving to be the most profitable. At the same time, some of the trading licenses became so important that they required a separate business unit, most notably those under International Motor Mart. Because of the success of the estates and the trading business, the family felt it would be useful to establish a separate company to deal with the properties and buildings they owned. During all this expansion, the Karimjees kept an eye on their business traditions and made sure that the original trading company developed into a 'mother company'.

During this period, the majority of the Karimjees lived in Zanzibar, Dar es Salaam and Tanga. A growing number of children were educated in India and increasingly in the UK, especially after the Second World War. In this sense, the Karimjees slowly oriented themselves towards Western Europe, while maintaining their business and family contacts with the East. They developed into a large international elite, which stretched beyond India and Africa.

Tayabali and Yusufali were appointed to the Board of Directors of all companies and the associated companies abroad, serving as senior partners in the companies. In addition, Abdulla Karimjee, Akberali Adamjee and later Abdulkarim Karimjee became active members and managers. In the early 1950s, the total turnover of the companies was estimated at "several million pounds a year." [32] In addition, a number of smaller companies were formed, amongst them a trading branch in Bombay. As the sisal industry expanded, there was a need for the sisal growers to unite and speak as a united front to the government, the sisal dealers, etc. The Tanganyika Sisal Growers Association (TSGA), and the Tanzanian Sisal Marketing Association (TASMA) were the dominant organisations. Abdulla Karimjee played a prominent role in establishing these institutions.

CHAPTER 4 · FROM TRADES TO ESTATES 1925 – 1963

TABLE 1 DISTRIBUTION OF DIRECTORSHIPS IN KARIMJEE JIVANJEE & CO., 1950

The distribution of directorships in 1950 provides insight into how the family divided business responsibilities. Yusufali, Tayabali, Abdulla and Akberali held directorships in most of the major companies.

NAME OF DIRECTOR	PARTICIPATION IN OTHER COMPANIES
Yusufali A.K Karimjee	Karimjee Jivanjee Estates Ltd., Tanga
	Karimjee Jivanjee & Co. Ltd., Dar es Salaam
	Karimjee Properties, Ltd., Dar es Salaam
	International Motor Mart Ltd., Dar es Salaam
	Karimjee Trading Co. Ltd., Bombay
	Karimjee Properties Ltd., Bombay
Tayabali Hassanali Karimjee	Karimjee Jivanjee Estates Ltd., Tanga
	Karimjee Jivanjee & Co. Ltd., Dar es Salaam
	Karimjee Properties, Ltd., Dar es Salaam
	International Motor Mart Ltd., Dar es Salaam
	Karimjee Trading Co. Ltd., Bombay
	Karimjee Properties Ltd., Bombay
Abdulla Mohamedali Karimjee	Karimjee Jivanjee Estates Ltd., Tanga
	Karimjee Jivanjee & Co. Ltd., Dar es Salaam
	Karimjee Properties, Ltd., Dar es Salaam
	International Motor Mart Ltd., Dar es Salaam
	Karimjee Trading Co. Ltd., Bombay
	Karimjee Properties Ltd., Bombay
	Tanganyika Sisal Marketing Association Ltd., Tanga
	TASMA Finance Corporation Ltd., Tanga
Akberali Abdulhussein Adamjee	Karimjee Jivanjee Estates Ltd., Tanga
	Karimjee Jivanjee & Co. Ltd., Dar es Salaam

Sources: Family archives; distribution of directorships

A short history of *sisal*

Cut leaves being counted into bundles of 30s.

The sisal plant originated in Mexico. The country had banned the export of the plants in order to protect its growing sisal industry in the late 19th century. It was clear that the expanding market of agricultural products would increasingly require the sisal plant, which could be used to make twine, rope and bags. Despite the ban, it soon spread to Brazil, Florida and the Caribbean. The German planter Dr Richard Hindorff illegally imported the plant from Florida via Hamburg to German East Africa. Eventually he was able to bring 200 bulbils to Tanga in East Africa in the 1890s. Initially he tried to produce sisal in the Usambara Mountains (on the German Government's experimental agricultural farm at Derema, that was later bought by Karimjees), but the first successful attempts were achieved in Korogwe. Consequently, Korogwe is now regarded as the birthplace of the sisal industry in East Africa. Later, Messrs. Amboni Estates imported the first commercial sisal bulbils from Mexico in 1906. In the early 20th century, the German East African Company (DOAG) in present-day Tanganyika and the British colonial government in East Africa (Kenya and Uganda) were preoccupied with the plantation economy. It was generally believed that plantations were the only way to bring modern agricultural techniques to the colonies. To this end, experiments were conducted with all kinds of varieties of coffees, teas, cotton and sisal in order to find out which crop and which seeds would produce the best results. Sisal was to become the principal crop in the region. At the turn of the century it was the third largest commercial crop in the country after coffee and coconuts. In 1928 it became the principal cash crop of Tanganyika. And this is – as we have seen (pp. 59-61) – exactly when Karimjee Jivanjee & Co. entered the plantation economy.

With prices around 30-40 pounds sterling per ton, sisal exports grew rapidly during the 1920s, from 22,000 tons in 1923 to 62,000 tons in 1929. However, as a result of the depression in the 1930s, and the growing competition from other sisal-growing nations worldwide, (Brazil, Mexico, Kenya, Haiti, Mozambique) prices plummeted. During the great depression, it became clear that large efficient estates such as Amboni were able to make profits despite the unfavourable economic conditions. The Karimjees merely broke even, but the small high-cost producers could barely make ends meet. The sisal planters responded by forming an employers' organisation, which organised concerted wage cuts, and maintained control of estate wages and conditions for nearly 30 years. Its plans for cooperative marketing failed, as several large estates (from the UK) insisted on marketing their sisal themselves. Nevertheless in 1948, Abdulla Karimjee made sure that the locally financed growers formed their own Tanganyika Sisal Marketing Association (TASMA), to which some of the foreign firms later became members. At that time, Karimjee Jivanjee & Co. owned estates totalling 10,000 hectares and employed 20,000 labourers.

One of the major challenges was to train and teach workers to operate machinery. In his book on the sisal industry in Tanganyika, Sir Eldred Hitchcock, chairman of Bird & Co., the second largest sisal producer, writes: "On the average, 70 percent of the labour of the industry consists of settled family labour on or adjacent to the estates, and the policy is further to build this up. The high rate of indirect expenditure on African labour is necessary owing to the lack of response by the African to money incentives by means of higher wage rates related to output. It is a country where leisure counts more than cash." [33]

Amboni Estates were the largest sisal producers and were partially owned by London sisal merchants Wigglesworth & Co. Wigglesworth helped finance the estates and dealt with the shipping and marketing of the sisal from the moment it left the estate. Other estates relied on agents and shippers, such as Arbuthnot Latham, Dalgety, and Ralli Brothers to buy their sisal or transport it on their own account (for a fee) to Europe where it was offered to merchants. The only exception was Karimjee Jivanjee, which until 1940 marketed its own and some other Asian-produced sisal in London.[34] It was then the largest of the local independent sisal producers with an annual production of 10,966 tonnes of sisal fibre. Noorani Plantations and Tayabali Essaji Sachak were two other prominent Asian firms. These two Bohra families formed an alliance with the marriage of Anver Karimjee to Ruby Sachak.

Sisal, and therefore Tanga, was booming on the eve of the Korean War (1950 - 1953). Many countries feared that this could be the beginning of another World War. Numerous countries immediately panicked and bought up strategic commodities such as tea and coffee, as well as sisal. The price of sisal went up from Sterling £ 18 per ton - which already yielded a high profit - to almost Sterling £ 250 per ton. Within this relative short period, Tanganyika's sisal producers became millionaires, which is how they got the nickname 'Sisal Barons'. The boom didn't last very long, but long enough to amass enormous wealth in Tanga. Sisal also became known as 'the white gold of Tanganyika'.

Sisal was the principal raw material for making marine rope for the shipping industry until the late 1950s when polypropylene came into use for nylon and other synthetic ropes. Nylon marine rope was stronger and more durable, as opposed to sisal, which was more easily broken down by sea water and salty air because it is an organic fibre. Sisal is now of little economic importance, whereas it formed the backbone of Tanganyika's economy until the 1980s.[35] Sisal was the prime raw material for making agricultural baler twine and competed directly with polypropylene yarn.

TABLE 2 SISAL PRODUCTION OF TANGANYIKA BY PROPRIETORS IN 1954

OWNERSHIP	PRODUCTION IN TONS	PERCENTAGE OF TOTAL
British	55,228	30.98
Greek	53,160	29.83
Asian	45,321	25.43
Swiss	15,549	8.72
African (random sisal)	3,979	2.23
Dutch	2,994	1.68
Italian	1,200	0,67
German	819	0,46
TOTAL	**178,250**	**100,00**

Source: Hitchcock, Sir Eldred, *The Sisal Industry of Tanganyika*, reprinted from the Tanganyika Trade Bulletin, 1955, p. 5.

DEVELOPING A SISAL PLANTATION

In the pioneering days of the sisal industry, almost every phase of the production process had to be started from scratch. There was neither a 'sisal growing association' nor a 'school of sisal growing'. The first phase in this new venture was a phase of discoveries, trial and error, and making mistakes and starting over again. Most of the knowledge of growing sisal originated in Mexico and Florida, but in East Africa the plantation owners had to conduct their own experiments in order to identify suitable planting material. One way to shorten the learning curve was to hire managers from abroad.

CHAPTER 4 · FROM TRADES TO ESTATES 1925 - 1963

An international Harvester 'Brookville' 40 H.P. diesel engine hauling off a train of wagons with leaf to the factory.

A SHORT HISTORY OF SISAL

Even before seedlings (bulbils) could be planted, a lot of work had to be done. Much of the land that was acquired by the family consisted of bush. So the land had to be cleared. This was often difficult owing to the quantity and the size of the vegetation. Initially, this operation was performed by a large group of labourers using axes, 'pangas' and hoes (for rooting out stumps). This heavy labour continued to be demanding until 'bush-breaker' tractors were introduced in the 1950s. Wherever possible, the clearance was often done with bulldozers. But these bulldozers had to be imported and then brought to Tanga, or even upcountry. Often they had to construct their own dirt roads along old caravan tracks to reach the plantation. In other places the work had to be done by hand and with sawing machines and tractors.

After the land was cleared, experimental plots were created to select suitable planting materials. These young plants were then transferred to nurseries where they would grow into small plants. The small plants were replanted in the fields in a so-called 'double row system'. In this system, two rows of plants would be planted close to each other with a broad space between the rows. This made it easier for workers to access the full-grown sisal during harvesting and weeding. Each sisal plant has over 200 leaves, which grow outwards from the centre of the bole, with the outer ones turning downwards as the fibre they contain matures lengthwise in the leaf. These outer leaves are cut in cycles of around twelve months. The leaves were wrapped in bundles of 30 and then carried to the sides of the plot by the workers, where they were stacked in a square meter. From there they were transported to the factory for decortication, drying, brushing, grading and pressing into bales.

The leaves were often transported from the field to the factory along a private narrow gauge railway track, which was built and maintained by the estate. Initially, loaded trolleys were pushed along the tracks by manual labour, or occasionally by cattle-drawn trailers. Later, diesel locomotives were imported and transported to the plantations. If we try to imagine transporting these engines from Tanga to the estates, as distance which sometimes spanned more than 200-300 miles, we can imagine the pioneering spirit required to achieve this.

At the factory, the leaves were then fed into the decorticator. This was a machine for crushing the leaves to separate the fibres from the waxy leaf. The wet fibre was then washed, cleaned and dried in the sun. Drying the fibres was often a job for women, whereas men did the previous part of the production process. When the fibre was dry, it was taken to the 'Brush Room' where it was brushed to a soft clean sheen and graded. Sisal was exported in bales of approximately 200 kg, which were transported to the nearest port (Tanga, Dar es Salaam or Mtwara). From there it was exported. This whole process was managed by European overseers.

In other words, buying estates and developing the land was but a small part of running sisal estates. There had to be a viable return on investments made in transport equipment, agricultural machinery and tractors, trucks, railway tracks and locomotives, factory machinery. In addition each estate had to invest in diesel generators for power supply and electricity, water pumps and pipes for water supply and graders for making and maintaining roads as there was no basic infrastructure in these remote rural locations. In the early years of the plantation development, workers had to be motivated to move from subsistence farming to become wage earners, as this was a new way of life for them. Karimjees shifted to a new level of entrepreneurship, which went far beyond the original trading business.

Within the Karimjee family, it was Abdulla Karimjee who managed the Karimjee Estate business (see portrait). He was involved in the estates from the beginning and had learnt the 'ins and outs' of the business by working hard, often with two feet in the mud, 'learning on the job', making mistakes, and improving his knowledge, output and performance.

CHAPTER 4 · FROM TRADES TO ESTATES 1925 - 1963

Women spreading and checking the drying fibre.

A SHORT HISTORY OF SISAL

*Land clearance.
The quantity and size of the roots often makes it difficult to fell trees with a bulldozer.*

CHAPTER 4 · FROM TRADES TO ESTATES 1925 – 1963

Sisal six weeks after planting.

A SHORT HISTORY OF SISAL

Hand cultivation in a field planted using the double row system. The plants are about 14 months old.

Sisal poles bearing bulbils.

CHAPTER 4 · FROM TRADES TO ESTATES 1925 - 1963

Slashing off the sharp tip thorn.

A SHORT HISTORY OF SISAL

Cut leaves being counted into bundles of 30.

Track maintenance.

CHAPTER 4 · FROM TRADES TO ESTATES 1925 – 1963

African worker carrying a bundle of sisal leaves.

A SHORT HISTORY OF SISAL

An international Harvester 'Brookville' 40 H.P. diesel engine hauling a train of wagons with leaves to the factory.

CHAPTER 4 · FROM TRADES TO ESTATES 1925 – 1963

Leaves being fed onto the feed conveyor table.

Removing wet fibre from a Robey decorticator.

A SHORT HISTORY OF SISAL

CHAPTER 4 · FROM TRADES TO ESTATES 1925 - 1963

A general view of a decorticator at work with a load of wet fibre being carried to the drying lanes.

A SHORT HISTORY OF SISAL

CHAPTER 4 · FROM TRADES TO ESTATES 1925 - 1963

Sisal drying lanes.

A SHORT HISTORY OF SISAL

Dried fibre being sorted before brushing.

CHAPTER 4 · FROM TRADES TO ESTATES 1925 - 1963

Grading a handful of fibre before packing it to the baler.

Flume Tow being forked out from the flume waste.

A SHORT HISTORY OF SISAL

Bales are off loaded from lorries for loading into lighters at Tanga wharf.

CHAPTER 4 · FROM TRADES TO ESTATES 1925 – 1963

A SHORT HISTORY OF SISAL

Pay day at a sisal estate.

CHAPTER 4 · FROM TRADES TO ESTATES 1925 – 1963

Sisal planters inspecting an experimental plot.

PORTRAIT

ABDULLA MOHAMEDALI KARIMJEE
1899 - 1978

Abdulla Mohamedali Karimjee had one of the most entrepreneurial spirits of the Karimjee family. With very little formal education he became the sisal baron of Tanga. His natural charm and charisma enabled him to treat his workers, employees and managers as well as with the Governor of Tanganyika, HH Aga Khan and Princess Margaret equally. He crossed many geographical and social borders. He was a traveller who frequently visited Europe, but also went to Egypt and India. He stood up to his father and his uncle when he married the love of his life Kianga Rannigger, the daughter of a German planter. He eventually retired in Spain and passed away during his travels in Sharjah and was buried in Dubai in 1978.

His natural charm and charisma enabled him to treat his workers, employees and managers as well as with the Governor of Tanganyika, HH Aga Khan and Princess Margaret equally. He was invited to be a part of the Tanganyika delegation to attend the Coronation of her Majesty Queen Elizabeth II in 1953. He crossed many geographical and social borders. He was a traveller who frequently visited Europe, but also went to Egypt and India. He stood up to his father and his uncle when he married the love of his life, Kianga Rannigger, the daughter of a German planter. He eventually retired in Spain and passed away during one of his last travels in Sharjah and was buried in Dubai in 1978.

Abdulla was born in his father's (Mohamedali) house above the head office of Karimjee Jivanjee & Co. Ltd. in Zanzibar in 1899. He went to primary school on the island. Unlike many other Karimjees, he was not sent for further education to the Alidina Visram High School in Mombassa nor to India or Britain. In Zanzibar, Abdulla was accustomed to a multi-ethnic environment. Swahilis, Arabs, Asians (Hindus and Muslims) and Europeans from all kinds of backgrounds lived in Stone Town and many visited his father's office regularly. He soon developed a nature that enabled him to relate easily to all of them.

Abdulla was born into a noble family but he was also a self-made man. The general family policy of many successful South Asian business families in East Africa was to send the son to another place to 'learn on the job'. The idea was that you gain more experience if you are forced to start from scratch yourself rather than rely on your family background. So, his father had sent him to Dar es Salaam when he was only 13 years old. Many Asians in Zanzibar opened shops and small businesses on the mainland as the East African interior became more developed. The Karimjees eventually opened their own office in Dar es Salaam in 1921. Apparently, around that time, Abdulla went to South Africa by 'piki piki' (a motorbike) to negotiate the deal with Caltex for the distribution of petroleum for the Tanganyika region, which was finalised in 1924. This illustrates his adventurous and bold approach 'to getting things done', which later served him well when he had to develop and manage the estates.

A young Abdulla Karimjee around 1917.

91

Abdulla Karimjee is honoured by his staff for his appointment as elected member of the Legislative Council in 1944.

After a few years his father Mohamedali decided that he was suitable for building the estate business. He managed the tea, coffee and sisal estates from the Karimjee office in Tanga. Abdulla built upon his father's business experience and developed it further. Abdulla differed from his father in three ways. First, he had travelled extensively and incorporated the changes he observed in other parts of the world into his economic decisions. He had a much more global mindset, whereas his father was more locally-oriented. Second, Abdulla managed the Karimjee Estates in East Africa-an organisation with more than 15,000 workers, including overseers, accountants, marketing people and agriculturalists. From this perspective, the head office in Zanzibar was a rather compact organisation. Third, he interacted freely with Europeans, Arabs, and Africans. He was close to workers, as well as to the leaders of the different societies and nations. He used his charm and charisma strategically to entertain his business friends and associates in Tanga.

In 1922 the Karimjees opened their plantation and estate offices in Tanga on the North East Coast of Tanganyika. The local economy was based on sisal, which had been brought to the colony several years earlier, and the population in the area grew rapidly. The town was also established as the terminus of the Usambara railway line, which runs inland to Moshi at the

CHAPTER 4 · FROM TRADES TO ESTATES 1925 - 1963

foot of Kilimanjaro. Tanga at that time was the premier port in Tanganyika. Most of the tea, coffee and sisal were exported from here. Abdulla started to develop the tea and sisal estates, which had been bought by his uncle Yusufali (see page 59-60). Without any prior experience, he learnt all about 'clearing the bush', planting and harvesting tea, coffee and sisal. He also learnt how to distinguish differences in quality and quantity, and how to sell the products produced. Some of the estates were up and running already, while others had to be developed from the ground up. He travelled a lot to the interior to visit the managers of the estates and he prepared the necessary production reports and financial statements. He made 'on site' decisions, for example he turned Derema Estate from a coffee estate into a tea estate in 1933. This was primarily due to coffee blight disease. A similar phenomenon was occurring in Ceylon at the same time. Tanga was barely developed when Abdulla arrived, but when he left in the 1960s the city had become the backbone of Tanganyika's export economy.

Abdulla had married Sukan, the first daughter of his uncle Yusufali. This was an example of more common marriage politics among Muslim business families throughout the world. Wherever small Muslim communities existed there was a growing tendency to intermarry. This was sometimes part of a strategy to maintain family wealth within the family. In line with this tradition, they married young and had children at a very early age. The first child, Hassan, was born in 1918. At that time, Abdulla was only nineteen and his wife sixteen. Three other children followed soon afterwards: Fiddahussein (born in 1920), Zehra (1923) and Shokat (1925). Abdulla was a loyal family man but he was exposed to different cultures, different ideas of family life and traditions and in the course of his life, he changed his orientation towards a more western lifestyle, while remaining a Muslim.

In 1926 he met Kianga Ranniger, the daughter of German

Abdulla portrait, around 1940.

farmers. They must have been settlers who were convinced that they would not return to Germany. This is supported by the fact that they named their daughter Kianga, which means 'rainbow' in Kiswahili. Kianga and Abdulla grew up close to each other. They shared the hard life of pioneers and estate builders in the bush. They dealt with the same challenges posed by the climate, travel and business. But most of all, Abdulla could not keep his eyes off the beautiful young Kianga.

We don't know what went through his young mind when he saw her. He fell in love, for sure. It was unclear how this should be dealt with. He was a very determined person, so he probably approached her directly. He was aware that a relationship with

Two women playing deck quoits.

Tayabali (left), Abdulla (right) Zehra (middle) and Kianga (sleeping), on a tour to Egypt.

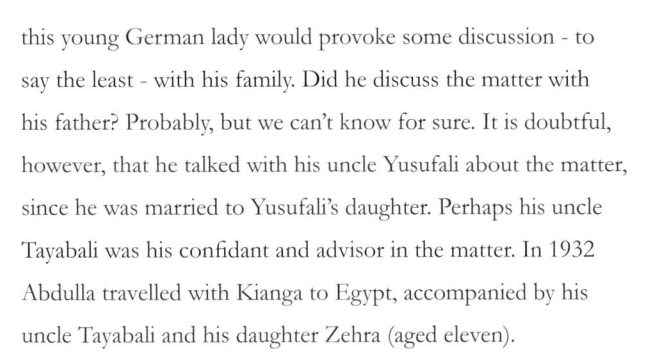

this young German lady would provoke some discussion - to say the least - with his family. Did he discuss the matter with his father? Probably, but we can't know for sure. It is doubtful, however, that he talked with his uncle Yusufali about the matter, since he was married to Yusufali's daughter. Perhaps his uncle Tayabali was his confidant and advisor in the matter. In 1932 Abdulla travelled with Kianga to Egypt, accompanied by his uncle Tayabali and his daughter Zehra (aged eleven).

In 1933, Abdulla married Kianga Ranigger, the love of his life. It was not unusual for Muslims of his standing to marry twice. Many Muslims married two, three or sometimes four times. The general practice in the higher Bohra circles was to re-marry when the original wife had passed away, leaving the father with children to look after, or in the exceptional case when the couple could not have children. But none of this applied to Abdulla. Thus, he went against convention and again made his own choice. He married again, while his wife Sukan was still alive. Moreover, he married a German (i.e. a white non-Muslim)

woman, who had to convert to Islam in order to marry him. This must have been an unusual situation for her and her parents as well. This was probably a way for Abdulla to show his family and his community that he was still a faithful Muslim and for her to show her love for him.

The marriage led to differences with his uncle Yusufali, who refused to talk to him after the marriage. The main reason for Yusufali taking offence was not the fact that this was a 'mixed marriage', as he himself was married to a Japanese woman, but because Abdulla's first wife Sukan was Yusufali's daughter and the mother of his grandchildren. The fact that Abdulla was running the estates that had been bought by Yusufali may well have complicated matters. In addition, Yusufali was still in charge of the export deals, especially those to Germany, which were very profitable just before the war. In short, the two avoided each other's company as much as possible.

The late 1930s were difficult for Abdulla and his wife Kianga. As Kianga had German parents, she had a German passport

CHAPTER 4 · FROM TRADES TO ESTATES 1925 - 1963

Abdulla was a keen hunter. The pictures show a hunting camp and Abdulla with his kill.

until 1937. The war between Germany and Britain impacted East Africa, as well. In 1940 Abdulla wrote a letter to the Governor of Tanganyika to request a British passport for her. These types of matters created a great deal of legal difficulties for the colonial officials. Initially, it was thought that the request was a straightforward one. If the marriage was legal and if Abdulla Karimjee was a British subject, his wife was a British subject as well. Therefore, she would be eligible for a British passport. Nevertheless, things turned out to be very confusing after they realised that it was not so clear that Abdulla was a British subject after all. Abdulla and his father Mohamedali were both born in Zanzibar. Zanzibar was not an official British colony or protectorate and therefore, Abdulla himself was not automatically a British subject. Nevertheless, on an earlier occasion, other colonial officials had issued him a British passport and it was difficult to withdraw that now. The exchange of legal letters does not provide clues as to the outcome, but the fact that Kianga was able to travel freely during the war as well as after it suggests that she also received a British passport. After the war they both did receive British Citizenship

Just after the Second World War, Abdulla had to use his influence and prestige to serve the Karimjee interests. He used a subtle silent diplomacy style to buy former German owned estates. At the start of World War II, all German properties and farms were taken over by the Custodian of Enemy Properties and leased to friendly allies to be managed on behalf of the government. The Karimjees were the only non-whites, who leased one of the estates, namely the Kisangara Sisal Estate. Nevertheless, after some time they were invited to manage the Tungi Sisal Estate in Morogoro as well. This estate was initially leased to Wigglesworth, but due to staff problems it was unable to run it properly.

After the war was over, a tribunal was appointed in order to sell these estates to those planters who had run them well. The Karimjees put in a bid for Tungi, Kisangara and one or two other estates. One of the Wigglesworth managers was overheard

96

CHAPTER 4 · FROM TRADES TO ESTATES 1925 - 1963

Abdulla and Kianga invited Abdulla's children and grandchildren to celebrate Christmas in Davos, Switzerland in the 1950s.

boasting at the Muthaiga Club in Nairobi that the Kisangara Estate was going to be sold to Wigglesworth. Amir Karimjee soon related this news to Abdulla Karimjee, the Managing Director of Karimjee Jivanjee Estates. Abdulla refused to believe that such treachery was possible and took no further action.

Nevertheless, when the tribunal met, all enemy sisal estates

A picture of the couple Abdulla and Kianga dancing in Davos in the 1950s. Davos was their favourite destination for winter sports.

were given to whites only, predominantly British companies. This was met with some furious reactions, notably from Sir Eldred Hitchcock, who was the managing director of Bird & Co., and a close friend of the family. He immediately complained to the Colonial Office in Whitehall. The Indian High Commissioner to Tanganyika, Shri Appa Pant, was also very upset about the matter. He approached the Karimjees and requested the consent of the Karimjee family to raise this issue in the United Nations.

Abdulla Karimjee, however, played the game differently. He realised that Asians lived under a colonial government and

Abdulla receives his Order of the British Empire (OBE) in 1961.

ABDULLA MOHAMEDALI KARIMJEE

1899	Born in Zanzibar
1917	Marries Sukan
1921	Junior assistant of Karimjee office in Dar es Salaam, visits South Africa by 'piki piki' to prepare the Caltex deal
1922	Opens plantation and estates offices in Tanga
1926	Meets Kianga Ranniger for the first time
1932	Travels with Kianga, Tayabali and daughter Zehra to Egypt
1933	Marries for the second time: Kianga Ranniger
1944	Member of the Tanganyika Legislative Council
1948	One of the founders of the Tanganyika Sisal Marketing Association
1955	Retires from active service, divides his time between London, Zurich, Torremolinos and Tanga
1956	Welcomes HRH Princess Margaret in Tanga
1961	Awarded OBE (Order of the British Empire)
1970	Advises his children to leave Tanzania because of exchange control
1978	Dies in Sharjah

that they could not afford to antagonise this institution. The 'silent lobbying' of the Karimjees worked. Out of appreciation for not embarrassing the colonial government, but rather condescendingly, Governor General Sir Edward Twining agreed to hand over the Kisangara Sisal Estate to the Karimjees.[37] However, Abdulla did not limit his appearances to Tanga alone. He established the Karimjees' London office, Karimjee Jivanjee & Co. (UK) Ltd. in 1955 with his younger brother Anver. This was a trading company that is still active. Mr Gordon, who had worked in Tanganyika as the custodian of enemy properties, was the first general manager. Abdulla's nephew Latif Karimjee now has a majority share and manages the company.

Abdulla became integrated internationally and frequently visited Europe where he spent many holidays in Davos, a famous ski resort in the Swiss Alps where all his children and grandchildren would join him at Christmas and New Year's. These visits were an eye-opener for his children and grandchildren as they would learn about European cuisine, improve their command of foreign languages and see how differently men and women interacted. They stayed in the prestigious Belvedere Hotel where they would have the same room and the same table at dinner every year. The grandchildren learned how to ice skate and ski, while Abdulla and Kianga went on walking tours. Abdulla also encouraged and facilitated his children's and grandchildren's education in Europe.

Photo of the official Tanganyika delegation to the Coronation, at 1956.

Back row: Canon R.M. Gibbons, CBE; Abdulla M.A. Karimjee, OBE; His Excellency Sir Edward Twining, GCMG, Governor General of Tanganyika; Chief Thomas Marealle II, Mangi Mkuru of the Chagga; E.C. Phillips, CBE.

Front row: Mrs Phillips; Mrs Karimjee; Lady Twining; Dr (Mrs) Gibbons: Mrs Marealle.

THE ROYAL CONNECTION

Abdulla was invited to attend the Coronation of Queen Elizabeth II, on 2 June 1953. The Coronation was attended by more than 8,000 people including Prime Ministers and Heads of State from around the Commonwealth. Abdulla Karimjee and his wife Kianga were part of the Tanganyika delegation. Among others, this delegation also included his Excellency Sir Edward Twining, GCMG, Governor of Tanganyika and Chief Thomas Marealle II, Mangi Mkuru of the Chagga (Chief of the Chagga tribe). With this invitation Abdulla represented the 'Asian population' of the Tanganyika Territory. This was an official recognition of Abdulla's own contribution to Tanganyika as well as the prominent status of the Karimjee family in general.

In September and October 1956, HRH Princess Margaret, sister of HM Queen Elizabeth II, went on a five-week tour to Zanzibar, East Africa and Mauritius. She visited Zanzibar and in Tanganyika she visited Ngorongoro Crater and Mount Kilimanjaro. She was welcomed in Dar es Salaam by Mayor Abdulkarim Karimjee. Next, she went to Tanga where she was welcomed by Abdulla Karimjee and Sir Eldred Hitchcock.

Princess Margaret was welcomed by (right to the left); Sir Eldred Hitchcock and Abdulla Karimjee OBE and other officials.

Princess Margaret visits Tanga in 1956.

The Red House Raskazone, Tanga in 1937.

The Spanish-Italian House built by Abdulla in the 1950s in Bombo, Tanga.

LIVING IN TANGA

Tanga used to be an important and prosperous town. After the sisal boom in the early 1950s, there was no city in Tanganyika that could match Tanga. There were two cinemas, a yacht club, a theatre, a library, several sports clubs and a swimming club. The city had an active and sophisticated cultural and business life. Imperial Airways Flying Boats (the predecessor of British Airways) stopped in Tanga and not in Dar es Salaam. In short, Tanga was booming.

Wealthy and well known in Tanga, Abdulla took the opportunity to loosen up the sectarian borders. As the yacht club was open to Europeans only, Abdulla started another club, the Raskazone Swimming Club. This club was open to Asians, Africans and Europeans alike.

And this was not the only time that Abdulla used his influence and prestige to break down social barriers. Another well known story in the family is that Abdulla used to travel between Dar es Salaam and Tanga by train. At that time, probably before the Second World War, non-whites were not allowed to travel first class. One day Abdulla asked for a first class ticket, the Goan ticket seller at Dar es Salaam train station stated that he would lose his job if he sold a first class-ticket to Abdulla. Abdulla replied that if he lost his job he would get a better-paid job at Karimjees. Abdulla got his ticket, the Goan did not lose his job and from then on no one was denied a first class ticket. Abdulla and other Karimjees were always ready to challenge the restrictive practices of the colonial government.

The Tanga of this epoch will be remembered for its parties. Sundowners, cocktails, dinners or banquets for between 20 and 400 guests were held every week. People would dance, eat, drink and party, especially in the Lead Memorial Hall. The women in the Karimjee family organised a clever distribution system, where each household was responsible for one or two dishes. In fact, as one woman recalls: 'we had a shared kitchen'. They all ran well-organised households in which excellently trained cooks prepared the dishes according to the wishes of all. The parties were attended by well-known people, like HH Aga Khan and Sir Edward Twining. When Abdulla & Kianga entered the room everyone turned to look at them. The charm and personality they shared always had a magnetic effect.

The Maweni house was a Garden of Eden built by Abdulla for Kianga's mother. The younger family members loved to get an invitation to spend some time there.

Abdulla built a gorgeous Spanish-Italian-style house in Tanga on a beautiful plot overlooking Tanga harbour. The quality of the materials used was unparalleled. The hardwood built-in cupboards, marble floors and wrought fittings are still intact as are the copper rain gutters.

This house - and Tanga in general - are still remembered fondly by Abdulla's children and grandchildren. They recall with great pleasure how Kianga taught them how to swim in the pool. Some of them went hunting and fishing, a leisure pursuit, which must have been passed down from their grandfather. Africa and 'estate life' awakens a 'hunter's spirit' in many males around the world and Abdulla was no exception. There are many pictures of him with his kill: a lion, a leopard, an antelope or a big game fish. Sometimes he hunted with

Raskazone Swimming Club, Tanga.

very wealthy and influential people like the Dutch Prince Claus and HH Aga Khan. After Abdulla retired, his younger brother Anver bought the house and lived there until it was nationalised in 1971. Soon after Kianga's father died Abdulla bought a gorgeous house in the Usambara Mountains very near to Kianga's family house. The Maweni house became the perfect retreat for Abdulla and his family. The house was located near Soni on the road to Lushoto and at the end of a peaceful valley. The house was named after the massive rock ('maweni' means stone or rock in Kiswahili). They dammed off the valley and created an artificial lake. In the middle of the lake they built a little island. Maweni was at an altitude of nearly 2000m and therefore had a very cool refreshing climate. This made it easier to keep a gorgeous garden, which made the place look like a Garden of Eden, complete with peacocks and tropical fruit. The inside of the house was like a German farmhouse with brickwork, fireplace and antique furniture. In short, it was a very warm and homely house with immaculate service and traditional European cuisine. All members of the Karimjee family looked forward to an invitation to Maweni. In the late 1960s and the early 1970s after most of the family had left Tanzania the house was maintained by Karimjee Jivanjee Estates. When the cost of maintenance was rising and the estates were operating at a loss, Abdulla was forced to give up the house and donated it to a German financed NGO doing rural development and community work in the Usambara Mountains. Currently a Swiss couple is running a guesthouse there.

CHAPTER 5

Political turmoil and economic decline 1964 - 1990

The three decades following the Independence of Tanzania were overshadowed by a growing political and economic insecurity among Asians in the country. All major events that took place in that time directly touched upon this issue. The Zanzibar revolution in 1964 eventually led to the migrations of the Asians to the mainland. The Asians felt the consequences of the Arusha Declaration in 1967 acutely, and the Nationalisation of Properties in 1971 and its economic consequences. The economic crackdown of 1984 was the last in a long line of adverse challenges to the business communities in Tanzania.

No one ever questioned the intentions of the various economic policies of CCM (Chama Cha Mapinduzi, i.e. Revolutionary Party) and President Julius Nyerere. Nyerere was credited with the fact that he had brought independence and unified the nation with one national language and had eliminated no tribal or racial barriers. Nevertheless, afterwards it was realised that most of the socialist economic policies did not fulfil their original promises. The economic policies needed to be revised. This eventually happened in the late 1980s.

During the Zanzibar Revolution in January 1964, several thousands of Arabs were killed while the number of Asian casualties was small. However, Asian shops were looted as well in this period. The revolution was basically a communist revolt, it also had racial underpinnings. With 300-600 armed men John Okello was able to overthrow the government and the feudal monarch Jamshid bin Abdullah Sultan of Zanzibar. This coup d' état between 18 and 20 January led to the massacre of 5,000 to 20,000 Arabs and Asians, whose families had been living in Zanzibar for centuries.[37] Little is known about this atrocity among the general public. Thousands more Indian and Arab people fled in fear of their lives, while their property was confiscated by the state. Many houses, buildings and factories belonging to the Karimjee family were confiscated. Most notably, the former head office of Karimjee Jivanjee & Co. Ltd. was converted into the People's Bank of Zanzibar. Sir Tayabali's house was taken over and first became the residence of the President, and later the Official Government Guest House.

Only three years later, on the mainland in 1967, Nyerere announced his famous Arusha Declaration. This marked the beginning of Ujamaa socialism in Tanzania. The principle of self-reliance, i.e. economic development based on the people's capacities and the country's resources, played a key role. The principles and the initial original implementation of the Arusha Declaration were well received, especially in the rural areas. New villages were built and there was hope in the eyes of many poor peasants in the country. Nevertheless, substantial economic results did not meet the expectations of the people. President Julius Nyerere and his political party TANU (Tanganyika National Union) felt that more drastic measures were necessary.

In the late 1960s and early 1970s, the state slowly took over control of the majority of the economic sectors, including foreign banks and insurance companies, and important industries and import/export firms. The government launched extensive programmes in the fields of business, trade and government to

The Karimjee Jivanjee main office in Zanzibar was nationalised and became the People's State Bank of Zanzibar in 1964.

replace Europeans and Asians with Africans wherever possible. Although the state was very dominant in the economy, there was always some flexibility left for private ventures, especially small and medium-sized ones. While the nationalisation of these economic sectors as well as of schools and buildings was not directed against the Asians specifically, Asians nevertheless were hit extremely hard, and it triggered a mass exodus of Indians in 1971. Some observers have estimated that 150,000 persons of Indian descent left the country and that the Indian population in Tanzania dropped by 60 per cent.[39]

The Acquisition of Buildings Act of April 1971 hit the Karimjee Jivanjee family hard. Although their sisal estates were not nationalised, numerous Karimjee buildings in Dar es Salaam and Tanga were. Almost overnight the family lost more than 35 buildings and houses in Dar es Salaam (see list in appendix). This did not include the buildings in Tanga, Moshi, Arusha, Mwanza, Mtwara, Lindi, and in many other places (probably more than 15). In many cases the Karimjees became tenants of the Registrar of Buildings or the National Housing Corporation (NHC). They had to rent their 'own' buildings. But the new landlord was unable to maintain the buildings at the most basic level. Some buildings fell into disrepair within months. The administrative procedures used for managing the nationalised properties were complex and multi-faceted. Ironically, in some cases the Office of the Registrar of Buildings requested that the Karimjee Jivanjee family assist in the process, for example with regard to the responsibilities of tenants and owners.

These major political changes and events coincided with major changes in the Karimjee management. The founders Hassanali, Mohamedali, Yusufali and Tayabali died or slowly retired and stepped down. Of the new generation, Abdulla, Abdulkarim, Akber Adamjee, Alibhai, Adam, Amir, Abdulkader, Hasan, Abid, Anver and Hakim Adamjee deserve mention. Nevertheless nearly every male family member worked in the family business from 1951 to 1971. It was out of a sense of duty that everyone played his or her part. Yusufali retired in Dar es Salaam, while his son Abdulkarim was managing director of

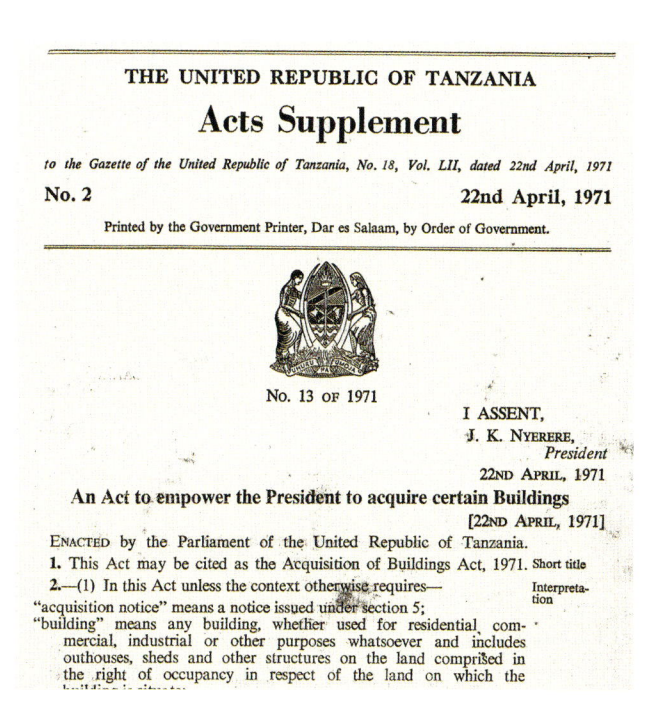

The page of the official Acquisition of Buildings Act of 1971.

Euro-Asians given three months to go

Asians arrive in UK with sad stories to tell

Asians head for Dar after Mombasa says 'No'

Asians from Uganda can't settle here — Maswanya

THE NATIONALIST
FREEDOM AND UNITY

Tanzanians mark third Arusha Declaration anniversary

MORE TAKE-OVERS THIS YEAR —NYERERE

Kawawa reminds

Identify yourselves Giri tells Indians

Airlines plan Asian exodus from Uganda

Chaos threatens

48 hours to quit or else...

in E. Africa citizens or refugees

Bleak future for 'stateless' Asians

Africans now take over as they leave

Asian exodus begins

,000 Asians to go soon

100 British Asians stranded in Tanzania

KENYA ASIANS FACE MASS DEPORTATION

POLITICAL TURMOIL AND ECONOMIC DECLINE 1964 - 1990

IMM. After Abdulla retired from the plantation business, he was happy to leave the responsibility to his younger brother Adam. Adam was educated in Poona University and at Trinity College, Cambridge University. He studied law and qualified as a barrister. He went back to Tanga to join his brother Abdulla in the estates. Abdulla taught him the ins and outs of estate management. Unfortunately, Adam died young in 1961 - the only member of the family to be buried in Tanga having died nearby in Muheza.

In the 1950s Anver, Mohamedali's youngest son, joined Adam in the estates business. While Adam specialised in accounts and labour relations, Anver had a degree in mechanical engineering from Poona. He gained his initial business experience helping Abdulla establish the Karimjee London office. Then, in his early career in Tanzania, he designed some of the equipment used for sisal processing before getting more involved in management. Adam's death hit Anver very hard indeed, but he eventually took over the overall management of the estates. However, like so many others, the political environment led to his departure, along with his young family, in 1971.

His older cousin Amir Yusufali Karimjee who was educated at Trinity College in Dublin joined Anver and stayed for some time. Amir started his career in Dar es Salaam with Karimjee Jivanjee Estates and was in charge of the Dar es Salaam office. Later, he was transferred to Karimjee Properties and then went into public service. He eventually became Assistant Minister for Commerce and Industries, a post which he held from 1957 to 1959 in the first pre-Independence government of Tanganyika. He was the founder-chairman of Tanganyika Broadcasting Corporation in 1961. He relocated to Tanga after Adam's death to take over management of the estates, and finally retired in Spain in 1965. He received his OBE in 1961 for service to the community.

After Anver's departure in 1971 management of Karimjee Jivanjee Estates fell into the capable hands of Alan Barber,

Adam Karimjee's grave in Tanga.

who had worked for the company for many years as Head of Administration and now became General Manager. In 1974 the management of Karimjee Jivanjee Estates was once again in the family's hands when Hatim Karimjee, the older son of Amir Karimjee, was appointed Managing Director. He was the grandson of Sir Yusufali Karimjee and the first of his generation to enter the family business. He was educated at Harrow Public School, Brighton Technical College, and the International Business Institute in Leysin, Switzerland. He had joined the family business in 1966, where he started as a 'Bwana Shamba' or field assistant on the family's tea and sisal plantations. He resides in Dar es Salaam and is the current chairman of Karimjee Jivanjee Ltd., the family's holding company for its businesses in Tanzania.

Tayabali had only one daughter: Fizza. Her husband Hakim Adamjee was very active as General Manager of Karimjee Jivanjee & Co. Ltd. He worked closely with and supported the

TABLE 3 THE NEW GENERATION OF KARIMJEE MANAGERS

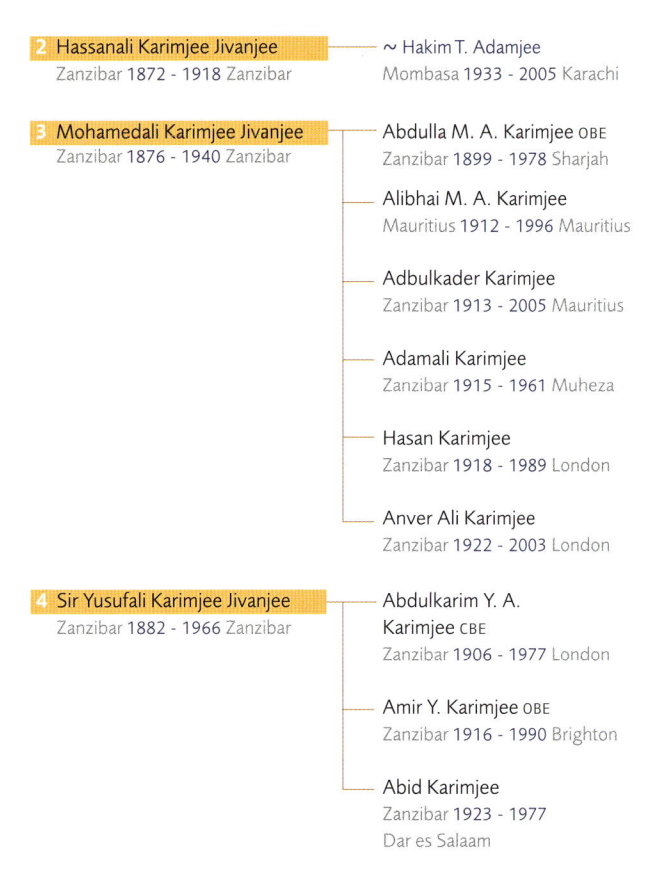

2 Hassanali Karimjee Jivanjee
Zanzibar 1872 - 1918 Zanzibar
— ~ Hakim T. Adamjee
Mombasa 1933 - 2005 Karachi

3 Mohamedali Karimjee Jivanjee
Zanzibar 1876 - 1940 Zanzibar
— Abdulla M. A. Karimjee OBE
Zanzibar 1899 - 1978 Sharjah
— Alibhai M. A. Karimjee
Mauritius 1912 - 1996 Mauritius
— Adbulkader Karimjee
Zanzibar 1913 - 2005 Mauritius
— Adamali Karimjee
Zanzibar 1915 - 1961 Muheza
— Hasan Karimjee
Zanzibar 1918 - 1989 London
— Anver Ali Karimjee
Zanzibar 1922 - 2003 London

4 Sir Yusufali Karimjee Jivanjee
Zanzibar 1882 - 1966 Zanzibar
— Abdulkarim Y. A. Karimjee CBE
Zanzibar 1906 - 1977 London
— Amir Y. Karimjee OBE
Zanzibar 1916 - 1990 Brighton
— Abid Karimjee
Zanzibar 1923 - 1977 Dar es Salaam

older Alibhai Karimjee who was managing director. Hakim intermingled with businessmen as well as politicians and was appointed a director of the State Trading Corporation after its establishment in 1969. Alibhai Karimjee the second oldest son of Mohamedali was very much the anchor of Karimjee Jivanjee & Co. Ltd. He served the family for nearly 50 years, first in Zanzibar and later in Dar es Salaam, mainly as managing director. He loved sports and there were many the photographs in the family albums showing Alibhai on the Cricket team or the Hockey team. Abdulla's two sons Hassan and Shokat lived in Tanga. Hassan Karimjee was responsible for all supplies for the tea and sisal estates, including oil and diesel, machinery parts as well as medicines for the estate dispensaries. He was also in charge of export shipping of tea and sisal from the estates and the country. Doctor Shokat Karimjee was a general practitioner who specialised in tropical medicine and was the company doctor. He had a surgery in Tanga and travelled extensively to all the estates. Yusufali's second oldest son Fazel Karimjee was less interested in sitting at a desk but had more friends in the Indian community than other family members. As a result he was valued for his in-depth market know-how and played an important role in identifying suitable consumer products for the family to import. Yusufali's youngest son Abid Karimjee made his career working in International Motor Mart Ltd in Tanga as well as in Dar es Salaam.

Initially, nationalisation of properties gave the Tanzanian middle class some hope for a better life as many believed that redistribution of wealth would benefit the poor. Many Asians however, were traumatised. Amir Karimjee, who was in charge of the properties at that time, was shocked at the nationalisation and left the country three days after it was announced. Others left the country for different reasons; Anver and Dr Shokat, for example, decided to leave the country because they had young children to educate. In short, most of the family members left the country, leaving behind only three 'die hards'. The most notable one was Abdulkarim, who believed that some of these extreme measures were temporarily necessary in order to create a better future for Tanzania. The other two die hards were Alibhai and the young man Hatim Karimjee (son of Amir Karimjee). At that time, Abdulkarim was running International Motor Mart (IMM), Alibhai was running the trading business Karimjee Jivanjee & Co. Ltd. and Hatim was running agriculture through Karimjee Jivanjee Estates Ltd.

Abdulkarim passed away in 1977. He had been the head of the family and the business in Dar es Salaam. Therefore,

POLITICAL TURMOIL AND ECONOMIC DECLINE 1964 - 1990

there was now an urgent need to bring in management for IMM. Fortunately, Anver Karimjee was willing to take up the responsibility now that his older children had finished school. He returned from Mauritius in 1978 with his wife and their youngest child, joining Hatim and Alibhai in the management of the family businesses. The Tanzanian economy remained weak and the business environment hostile. No one could have known that the worst was yet to come. The late 1970s witnessed the war with Uganda when Idi Amin invaded northwestern Tanzania. This was also the period when oil prices rose sharply. Although Tanzania won the war with Uganda, the toll it had taken, in addition to the high oil prices, caused the economy to collapse. Years of economic and social hardship followed.

The hardship peaked with the "Economic Sabotage Crackdown" in 1983. The outer signs of economic deterioration were evident everywhere. There were long lines early each morning in Dar es Salaam outside a medium-sized bakery for white bread. There was a shortage of almost all consumer staples: flour, cooking oil, sugar, kerosene, charcoal and clothing. For the first time some residents spoke privately of the possibility of urban violence. The government's policies did not secure a minimum amount of food for the majority of the urban population. As for the rural population, there was virtually nothing to buy.

The silent dissatisfaction and the withdrawal from the official market to the black market reinforced government belief that shortages of goods had been deliberately brought about through hoarding, with the objective of subverting the government. The nationalisation measure of 1967 and 1971 had affected traders and businessmen, in particular. There were suspicions that the emerging economic elite made up of successful Asian businessmen, powerful African bureaucrats and politically dissatisfied politicians was conspiring with self-exiled dissidents, especially from Zanzibar, to bring about riots and chaos. In April 1983, more than 1000 people were arrested. Although only 23 were Asians, it significantly increased the feeling of insecurity among Asians in Tanzania. The stories about this dark period in East African history are more about survival than about business development. This was a time of acute shortages of foreign exchange and raw materials and nearly all basic and essential consumer products. Overseas visitors were asked to bring bread, soap, toothpaste, light bulbs and toilet paper instead of a customary bottle of Scotch whisky or French perfume. Sometimes people got lucky when a visiting ship of the German East Africa Line or a friendly Ambassador gave them a bottle of wine or a few cans of imported beer. During the difficult crackdown period, further family departures led to Anver Karimjee having to take on management responsibility for both Karimjee Jivanjee Estates and IMM, by then the two remaining family-owned businesses in Tanzania. He made frequent, regular trips to Tanga as well as visits to individual plantations, in addition to his work and travel for IMM. He often took his wife Ruby with him on these trips; he was now in his sixties, and the effort of holding both businesses together took its toll on his health.[39]

One striking story reveals the increased uneasiness of that time. One day, after Alibhai and Shirin had left to retire in Mauritius, Alibhai's former houseboy Haroun told Anver that there was a gun in Alibhai's house. This was a very dangerous matter - the family risked severe repercussions if the gun was found. Having a gun could be interpreted as an act against the government. Anver was grateful that Haroun did not report the matter to the police, but he had to find a solution for the gun. Anver and Ruby decided to bury it in a small forest behind some trees in the night. They went there together to get the job done. This turned out to be one of the most frightening experiences of their life. The government had told the populace, repeatedly, on the radio and in the newspapers, to be vigilant of economic saboteurs and, as a result, everyone lived in an atmosphere of fear.

PORTRAIT

ABDULKARIM YUSUFALI KARIMJEE
1906 - 1977

Abdulkarim was another remarkable member of the Karimjee family. He exhibited all the qualities that the Karimjee family had acquired over the previous generations. As a businessman, politician and true Tanzanian, he was a shrewd entrepreneur with an eye for new developments and options. He was Mayor of Dar es Salaam five times, a prominent member of the colonial legislative council and the first Speaker of the Parliament after independence was declared. In fact, he presided over the independence ceremony in 1961. He assisted his country as well as his family in difficult times in the late 1960s and the early 1970s. His life story reads like a long tale of special occasions, nominations and interesting, influential jobs and positions.

Abdulkarim was born on 15 February 1906 and was the first surviving son of Yusufali. Like the other Karimjees of his generation, he received his primary education in Gujarati and Arabic in Zanzibar. He was sent for further education to Burhangpur, India in 1917, where he took English for two years, but returned to Africa at the age of 13 because he was in poor health. In 1919 he became a trainee in the head office in Dar es Salaam under the supervision of Mr Akberali Adamjee, who was the manager at the time.

In 1930 he married Batool Noorbhai Jafferjee from Karachi. The young couple settled in Dar es Salaam, where Abdulkarim started to work for the head office. He was primarily in charge of the import/export department as well as the agricultural business. He travelled extensively, visiting Germany and the UK frequently before the Second World War. In those days very few South Asians from Africa visited Europe. Therefore, he became an important cultural broker in Africa by introducing European political and economic standards of service and efficiency. Combining Asian, African and European worlds he was often able to bridge differences in political and economic affairs.

When the Second World War began, Abdulkarim went to Bombay and opened a trading office, exporting textiles to East Africa and importing cloves from Zanzibar. Despite the war the family was able to run the business successfully. In 1943 Abdulkarim travelled on a British troopship to Madagascar, where his sister Husseina and brother-in-law Abdulla (originally from Mauritius) lived for a few years. Since the war years, there had been no news of them (Madagascar, being a French colony, fell under the Vichy government). Travelling during wartime was extremely difficult and dangerous, but Abdulkarim used his contacts to get permission to travel from Dar es Salaam to Madagascar. This visit is still remembered vividly by the Mauritius side of the family who were in Madagascar during the war years, as it was the first time they had received news from East Africa.

After the war he took his wife Batool and two daughters on a 'Tour of Europe', including Switzerland, France, Spain and the UK in 1952. At that time, Abdulkarim had visited Europe

Wedding picture Zanzibar 1930; Abdulkarim Karimjee and Batul Noorbhai (left) and Abdulla Currimjee and Huseina Karimjee (right).

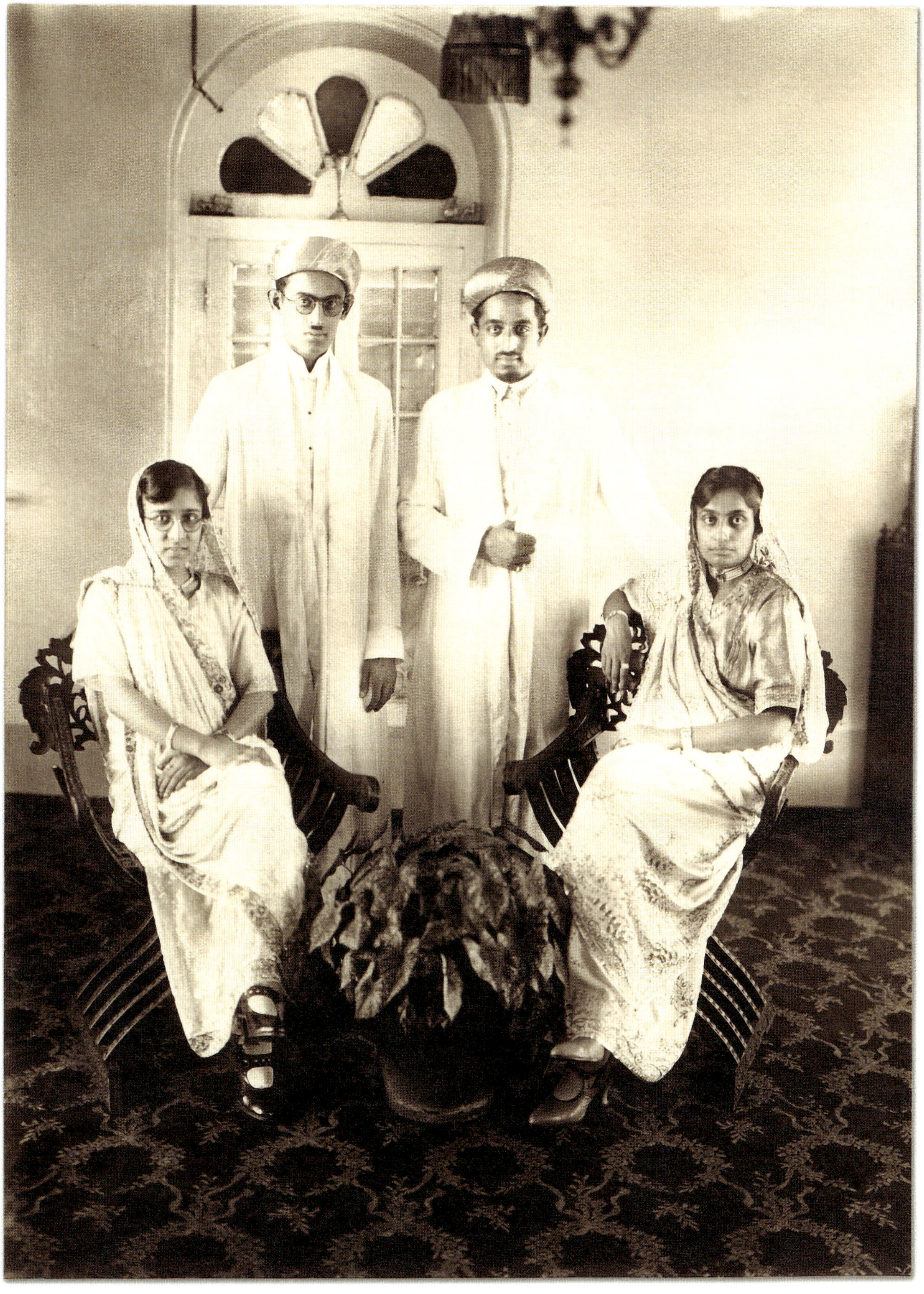

Wedding picture at the 'double wedding' of Abdulkarim and Batul and Abdulla and Huseina, Zanzibar the 8th of May, 1930. At this day the Karimjees and the Currimjees (the KJs and the CJs) were literally married together.

Back row, standing, left to right; Children of Yusufali: Hatim, Shirin, Fazal, Amir, Rubab; son of Abdulla and Sukan, Hasan.

Middle row, seated, left to right; Abdulla Currimjee (of Mauritius), Huseina (his wife), Sukan (wife of Yusufali), Abdulkarim, Batul (wife of Abdulkarim), Yusufali, Sukan (daughter of Yusufali and wife of Abdulla Karimjee), Abdulla.

Seated on Floor, left to right; Children of Yusufali; Abid, Zainab. Fidahussein (son of Sukan and Abdulla), Zehra (Daughter of Sukan and Abdulla), Shokat (son of Sukan and Abdulla).

many times before, dealing with the Rootes Group in the UK. He encouraged his children to study at private schools in Europe (especially Switzerland), which they did. The idea was that they would meet all kinds of children from all over the world. Learning French was an important aspect of their upbringing as world citizens.

In that year he was awarded a CBE (Commander of the British Empire) for his service to the people. This may have led to his increased interest in 'public affairs', especially municipal affairs. He was Deputy Mayor of Dar es Salaam in 1952 and 1956, and Mayor in 1951, 1954 and 1957. As Mayor he made friends with the British administration but more importantly he developed contacts and friendships with prominent Africans who many years later were to play a vital role in the independence movement. As Mayor he recognised the absence of a Town Hall

CHAPTER 5 · POLITICAL TURMOIL AND ECONOMIC DECLINE 1964 – 1990

Abdulkarim left the Legislative Council in 1962 and was given a prolonged round of applause lasting several minutes.

and persuaded his father Sir Yusufali Karimjee to make the single largest donation that the Karimjee family had ever made by building Karimjee Hall and donating it to the Municipal Council of Dar es Salaam in 1955. After independence was declared, Karimjee Hall was used for nearly 40 years by Parliament until the new Parliament House was built in Dodoma, Tanzania's capital. The Mayor's office and the City council chamber still meet at Karimjee Hall.

These were interesting times. The independence of Tanganyika was foreseeable and a topic of constant debate. Julius Nyerere was the leader of TANU (Tanganyika African National Union). A consistently recurring debate related to how the country should develop. Would a more 'capitalist' approach be chosen, as in neighbouring Kenya ? Or was a more socialist approach preferred? We now know, TANU chose for the latter

---

TANGANYIKA STANDARD, December 9, 1961.

A message from... THE SPEAKER

Mr. A. Y. A. KARIMJEE

I am proud to be Speaker of our National Assembly at this turning point in the history of Tanganyika and to be able to send you my personal message of good will.

The National Assembly, whom you elected, has amply justified the trust you placed in its Members.

Led by our Prime Minister, Tanganyika has not only won its freedom but also the respect, the confidence and indeed the admiration of all the nations of the world who have so warmly welcomed her to the United Nations Organisation.

In seeking to maintain the peace, order and good government of Tanganyika through democratic principles and the rule of law, our Assembly aims at the highest form of civilisation known to man—a State in which everyone can pursue his legitimate undertakings without fear or favour, in the knowledge that in his dealings with the Government he will meet with justice.

Personally, I am confident that with united effort and hard work our country will reap the full benefit of its Independence.

To see this take place is my most fervent desire.

I pray for the peace, progress and prosperity of Tanganyika.

Abdulkarim Karimjee

Abdulkarim Karimjee cited at length in the Tanganyika Standard 9th December 1961.

course. Abdulkarim certainly played his part in the informal discussions about these issues.

Adbulkarim's most prestigious post, however, was that of Speaker of the Tanganyika Legislative Council. It was established under the Tanganyika Legislative Council Order and Council, a law enacted by the British Parliament in 1926. The Council had 20 members, all appointed by the Governor. Abdulkarim had been nominated as a Member of the Tanganyika Legislative Council in 1949 and was appointed Deputy Speaker in 1954. The primary change to the Legislative Council was implemented in 1953 when the First Speaker was appointed to replace the Governor as chairman of the council. The Speaker took office on 1 November 1953. The second major change was in 1958 when a few members, who had been elected by the people, were added to the Council. This was the earliest election to be allowed in the colony and it was the first time political parties – that were already registered – were allowed to participate in elections.

Abdulkarim was invited by the Commonwealth Parliamentary Association to attend a month's course in parliamentary procedure and practice in the Houses of Parliament at Westminster and at Stormont, Northern Ireland in 1956. He demonstrated his grasp of parliamentary procedure particularly during the final months of 1957 and in 1958, when he was Acting Speaker in the absence of Sir William Scupham. In 1959 he was appointed Speaker of the Tanganyika Legislative Council. When Tanganyika became independent, he was Speaker of the first parliament, which met in Karimjee Hall in 1961. He presided over the ceremony in which Tanganyika received its independence. This definitely must have been one of the highlights of his impressive career. By then he had seen the House change from a nominated body to an elected one. In addition, its membership had increased from 29 to 81. He left the House in 1962 and was given a prolonged round of applause lasting several minutes.

Abdulkarim continued his public career after independence was declared. He became director of National Development Corporation (NDC), and National Bank of Commerce (NBC) and was vice chancellor of University College Dar es Salaam from 1961 to 1970, the predecessor of the present University of Dar es Salaam. He also negotiated an agreement to establish the Tanzania National Library, the main library in the country to this day. It was founded with a donation of £65,000 by the Karimjees and a matching grant from the government.

During the events of 1967 (Arusha Declaration, see page 104) and 1971 (acquisition of buildings see page 107), he had become so involved in politics that he felt duty-bound to stay in the country. He shared his tremendous experience in politics with Julius Nyerere, who became a close friend. In fact, Nyerere visited his home for the first time after the war. They often shared their thoughts at Abdulkarim's house in Dar es Salaam in the evening after a long working day. He very much agreed with Nyerere that the well-to-do and well-educated people of East Africa were obliged to share their knowledge and wealth with the disadvantaged people. At the same time, however, Abdulkarim advised his family members to leave the country especially those with younger children. He felt that, for the time being, the future of the Karimjees was not in Africa. He foresaw difficult times ahead for Asians in East Africa. Nevertheless, he himself maintained his position of serving the country.

Meanwhile, Abdulkarim, was still the managing director of IMM and did not neglect that responsibility. Except for the supervision of daily affairs, he was aware that strategic opportunities would contribute to the wealth of the family. His most important contribution in this respect was his involvement in acquiring the Toyota franchise, which is still one of the most important money-spinners of the Karimjees. The deal with Toyota is a good example of three important pillars of successful businessmen coming together: i.e. (A) having a good

CHAPTER 5 · POLITICAL TURMOIL AND ECONOMIC DECLINE 1964 – 1990

The Karimjee family meets Julius Nyerere in front of the TANU building in Tanga in 1966.
From left to right; Abid Karimjee, Amir Karimjee, Mrs Bilquis,, Mrs Munira Shokat Karimjee, Julius Nyerere,
Dr Shokat Karimjee, Anver Karimjee, Mrs Ruby, Alibhai Karimjee, Hakim Adamjee.

Abdulkarim meets Princess Margaret in Dar es Salaam in 1956.

name; (B) using one's entrepreneurial instinct, and (C) being in the right place at the right time. These ingredients make up the unique criteria for closing the 'deal of the century'.

The Toyota story began in Rhodesia when Prime Minister Ian Smith issued a Unilateral Declaration of Independence (UDI) from Britain in 1965. The British government was offended by this one-sided approach and decided to impose economic sanctions against Rhodesia. In particular they imposed a blockade on shipments to Rhodesia especially through Beira, Mozambique. The Toyota agent in Rhodesia was Mobile Motors, owned by the Friend family (in the 1980s they were taken over by Lonrho: the London and Rhodesian Company, established in 1909). Toyota had sent a ship full of Toyotas to Beira for delivery to Rhodesia and due to the British blockade the ship eventually arrived in Dar es Salaam under strict orders not to transship to Rhodesia.

Thus, the Friend family with Toyota Tsusho Corporation company were looking for an agent in Dar es Salaam to sell these cars locally and prevent further losses. In those days Japanese products were considered 'cheap products', like cheap Japanese toys, etc. They eventually approached IMM. Abdulkarim consulted his right-hand man Pitamber who was officially his secretary, but in many ways acted as executive manager. IMM agreed to take the vehicles on a consignment basis in which case they would pay the Friends only after the vehicles were sold.

The Karimjees saw that the cars were very popular. Toyota quality was not as good as that of American and British cars, but the cars were fully equipped with accessories and attractive gadgets, like short-wave radios with electric antenna which could receive the BBC World Service, as well as with cigarette lighters, wing mirrors, etc. These accessories were available at an additional fee in British cars but were standard features in Toyotas. As a result, the first consignment sold very rapidly. This may have been partly due to Abdulkarim's unique sales strategy whereby he selected some wealthy clients, registered the Toyotas in their name without their knowledge and delivered the cars to them with an "invoice". The strategy worked, as no one refused to accept Abdulkarim's 'gift'. The Karimjees may have foreseen that British cars were on their way out due to rising cost of production, and increasing interference by British trade unions, making British cars too expensive as well as unable to provide customer service. The Karimjees applied for and received the Toyota agency from Toyota Motor Corporation. International

Motor Mart became Toyota's fourth agency in Sub-Saharan Africa after agencies in South Africa, Sudan and Rhodesia.

In the late 1970s, Abdulkarim had moved to a small apartment in Dar es Salaam. He had lived in big houses, but now he felt that a small flat was enough. One day he was doing some small repairs in his house and while changing a light bulb, he slipped and fell. Although it was just a minor accident, he went to his doctor D. N. Patel for a check-up. The doctor was not satisfied with the results and advised Abdulkarim that he should go to London for further checks.

Abdulkarim must have felt that something was wrong. Family members remember that prior to leaving for London he took great care in winding up his affairs. For example, he used to go to the hairdresser near the office and as he rarely kept cash in his pocket, he settled the accounts with the hairdresser every six months or so. But after the visit with the doctor, he made a point of going there to settle his accounts. He also summoned his nephew Hatim Karimjee who was working as an Executive Assistant and told him that it was time to brief him on his Japanese grandmother's affairs, about the various family trusts and about various charitable issues. He had never informed Hatim about these issues before. In short he was clearing his desk.

After this briefing he went to London and he was admitted to Princess Grace Hospital for a biopsy. On the 7th September 1977, he went to the Royal Free Hospital for further examination. While he was on the examination table, he had a massive heart attack and passed away. He was buried two days later on the 9th September of 1977 in Brookwood Cemetery, near Greater London. This was one of the first cemeteries in Europe to have a separate plot for Muslim burials, around the 1860s.

ABDULKARIM KARIMJEE

1906	Born in Zanzibar
1917	Education in India
1919	Starts to work for the head office in Dar es Salaam
1930	Marries Batool Noorbhai Jafferjee of Karachi
1939	Opens a trading branch in Bombay (closed in 1977)
1952 - 1958	Member of the East African Central Legislative Council, awarded a CBE (Commander of the British Empire)
1961	First Speaker of parliament in an independent Tanzania
1961 - 70	Chairman of the University College of Dar es Salaam
1965	Acquires license with Toyota
1973	Receives the Degree of Doctor of Law at the University of Dar es Salaam 'honoris causa'. Appointed chancellor in October
1977	Dies in London, buried in Brookwood Cemetery

Abdulkarim's grave at Brookwood Cemetery.

A HOUSE IN DAR ES SALAAM

One of the most beautiful homes in Dar es Salaam is the so-called 'Spanish house', the current residence of the Ambassador of Italy. The 'Spanish house' is inspired by the Alhambra at Granada and the Palace of King Alfonso XIII in Seville. The house is built around a courtyard with a fountain in the middle. Inside there are Spanish tiles, wrought iron grills, and wooden panels containing verses from the Koran as well as references to Spanish kingdoms. Amir Karimjee built this marvellous villa between 1950 and 1952. The architect was his close friend Tigger Hastings, and it is well known that Amir himself contributed considerably to the project. Amir had visited Spain and collected numerous photographs of historic buildings. He provided advice about the design, the colours and the materials to be used. Some of the materials were imported directly from Andalusia, like the majolica tiles and the wrought-iron gates and gratings. In the garden stands a Buddha tree (Abo tree or Peepul), transplanted by

The north and the south wings of the Spanish house built by Amir Karimjee.
It is currently the residence of the Italian Ambassador in Dar es Salaam.

Spanish house: Wood panels with excerpts from the Koran.

The stairs of the north wing tiled in Andalusian majolica.

a Buddhist monk in 1952 from Ceylon. This huge tree with dome-shaped foliage has a diameter of thirty meters and a wide twisted trunk intertwined with robust boughs. Amir's wife Kulsum who came from Ceylon provided the inspiration for the idea. The villa is divided in two wings that are connected by a quadrangular courtyard. The north wing covers two floors and has a loggia. The staircase is lined with Andalusian majolica tiles. The south wing consists of a large lounge illuminated by 20 skylights and six French windows. Among the guests who stayed or visited the Spanish House are the likes of HH Aga Khan, Prince Aly Khan, Louis Armstrong, the British Governor General Edward Twining and Richard Turnbull as well as Julius Nyerere and Bernhard Grizmek, who is famous for the film 'Serengeti Shall Not Die'. Amir sold the house in 1963 to the Italian State and it is still the residence of the Italian Ambassador.

The famous Abu tree or Peepul (Buddha tree) was planted by a Buddhist monk from Ceylon in 1952. Recently, the Italian Ambassador had to move the Italian flag to allow the tree more space to expand.

In 1985, Ali Hassan Mwinyi was elected President, succeeding Nyerere. Soon thereafter, the government reached an agreement with the International Monetary Fund, World Bank and other donors to introduce an 'Economic Recovery Programme'. The programme comprised the standard elements of structural adjustment programmes, including devaluation, liberalisation of external trade, the elimination of price controls and subsidies, and a reduction in state expenditure. It also provided for the end of the one-party state and the beginning of a multi-party democracy.

Tanzania needed an 'Econimic Recovery Programm', but so did the Karimjee Jivanjee business. Ater years of bad economic conditions, limited manpower and lack of investment, the businesses were facing serious challenges. The business was in a shocking state. Toyota sales and profits were very low. There was a shortage of qualified management and skilled technicians. Toyota themselves was hinting that unless the company was turned around rapidly, it would look for a new distributor in Tanzania. Tea and sisal production was very low and Karimjee Jivanjee Estates was operating at a loss. Due to the national shortage of foreign exchange as well as the accumulated losses, there was no money to replace tractors and pumps, repair factory machinery and as a result of shortages of consumer goods in the shops, workers had no incentive to pick tea or to cut sisal. Without workers to harvest crops, farms ultimately collapse. In 1986 Azim Karimjee (Abdulla's grandson, and a qualified Management Consultant based in London) was invited to Dar es Salaam together with Saleem Karimjee (Anver's son), to advise Anver on how to revitalise the family businesses.

From 5 to 8 April 1987 the Karimjee family convened a series of meetings in Mauritius to decide on the future of their business in Tanzania and how to reverse the acute decline. Ten shareholder representatives were present namely Alibhai & Shirin, Anver, Fazel & Batul, Abdulkader, Hakim, Hatim, Latif,

TABLE 4 MAJOR SHAREHOLDER MEETING 1987

2 Hassanali Karimjee Jivanjee
Zanzibar 1872 - 1918 Zanzibar

— Fizza Karimjee
Karachi 1937
~ Hakim T. Adamjee
Mombasa 1933 - 2005 Karachi

3 Mohamedali Karimjee Jivanjee
Zanzibar 1876 - 1940 Zanzibar

— Alibhai M. A. Karimjee
Mauritius 1912 - 1996 Mauritius
~ *Shirin Karimjee*
Zanzibar 1914 - 2002 Mauritius

— Adbulkader Karimjee
Zanzibar 1913 - 2005 Mauritius

— Anver Ali Karimjee
Zanzibar 1922 - 2003 London

— Latif Karimjee
Karachi 1948

4 Sir Yusufali Karimjee Jivanjee
Zanzibar 1882 - 1966 Zanzibar

— Fazal Karimjee
Zanzibar 1912 - 1992 Mauritius
~ *Batul Karimjee*
Zanzibar 1918 - 2002 Mauritius

— Mustan Currimjee
Zanzibar 1936
~ *Rosemine Karimjee*
Dar es Salaam 1939

— Hatim Karimjee
Zanzibar 1945

Mustan and Rosy Currimjee. In addition three senior members of the Currimjee family were present to assist and advise, namely Carrim, Bashir and Fakhru.

Various proposals were considered including one to sell out to Comcraft the investment holding company of the Chandaria family. They were looking to diversify their investments in East Africa and foresaw changes in government policies. In fact they had signed a Memorandum of Understanding and were waiting for shareholders' approval. This approval never came.[41] Currimjee Jivanjee family, otherwise known as CJ - as opposed to KJ for Karimjee Jivanjee - also made a proposal for a joint venture investment with KJ to avoid disposing the business to outsiders. After four days of deliberations the family decided not to sell and to invite Hatim Karimjee to re-join the family business to head the revitalisation of Karimjee Jivanjee Estates and International Motor Mart. The family believed that the time was right because government policy had changed after 1985 and a new economic era was dawning.

In Mauritius agreement was reached to streamline the family's shareholdings into a single holding company and that all other operating companies of Karimjee Jivanjee Estates and International Motor Mart would become wholly owned subsidiaries of the holding company Karimjee Jivanjee Limited (Originally named Karimjee Jivanjee (1825) Ltd.). Hakim Adamjee was appointed Chairman and Mustan Currimjee, Hatim Karimjee, Latif Karimjee and Saleem Karimjee were elected Directors. Hatim became the managing director. This was an important step in the new era of the Karimjee Jivanjee business. The new order was designed to restore transparency and trust. Several older directors retired and the torch was handed down to the next generation.

Work to rehabilitate the family business began in earnest in 1988. The immediate focus was on International Motor Mart where Hatim successfully repositioned the relationship with Toyota, improving the ability of the business to capitalise on the rapidly rising demand for new cars following liberalisation. This development was quickly followed up with a strategy to strengthen management, strengthen dealer network, further increase new vehicle sales and make improvements to after sales service. Toyota profits were channelled into agriculture to provide quick fixes to strengthen management, improve transportation and production machinery. Nevertheless it was an uphill struggle and shareholders were anxious for results especially for payment of dividends.

Hatim Karimjee gave an emotional speech during a shareholders meeting in London in 1989 where he promised to commence payment of dividends. One of his key concerns was to convince the shareholders who had not been to Tanzania in twenty years that Tanzania was changing. This was not the same Tanzania that they had left behind, because of the extreme form of socialism and nationalisations that had been introduced. Some family members were still feeling the effects of that experience. In addition, they had not enjoyed any dividends for many years and some of them were looking for an exit-strategy.

It soon became clear, however, that the business was in a transitional stage. One of the biggest challenges was to revive the tea and sisal businesses. Karimjee Jivanjee Estates, whose name was changed to Karimjee Agriculture in 1991, had consistently taken losses during the past 20 years. The tea group comprised two tea factories (Monga and Derema) and three field divisions (Monga, Derema and Maramba). The tea estates had a combined area of 5,300 hectares, of which 880 hectares was planted tea with a production capacity of 1,500 tons of made tea per annum. The sisal group comprised five sisal estates (Kisangara, Hasani, Fatemi, Alavi and Mikindani) located throughout Tanzania in the Kilimanjaro, Coast, Morogoro and Mtwara Regions.

By 1986 production had declined to 350 tons of tea and 1,425 tons of sisal. This was equivalent to a 23% capacity for tea and a 10% capacity for sisal. This was due to many factors such as labour shortages, lack of working capital, insufficient replanting, the worsening condition of machinery and equipment, lack of foreign exchange (e.g. to buy new machinery or spare parts), an overvalued currency, a punitive export tax, and the socio-economic upheaval arising from the government's nationalisation projects.⁴²

In 1989, Price Waterhouse Associates conducted a feasibility study, the conclusion of which was the following: "Our economic analysis shows that all the Karimjee Estates (both tea and sisal) are attractive propositions for rehabilitation." ⁴³ In addition it argued that the Karimjee estates would be able to repay external financing accepted for revitalisation. This was in a time when the government had accepted loans from the World Bank and the International Monetary Fund in exchange for liberalisation of the economy. The Karimjees had already received some funds from Cooperative Rural Development Bank (CRDB) for revitalisation and negotiations were started with the Commonwealth Development Cooperation (CDC).

Karimjee Agricultural, CDC and CRDB started an ambitious revitalisation program, worth over 10 million USD in 1991. CDC invested USD 6.1 million (equity and loan), the Karimjees invested USD 2.4 million equity, and CRDB issued a loan of 1.7 million USD. The objective of the programmes was to increase the production levels of tea to 2,000 tons and of sisal to more than 10,000 tons per annum, mainly by modernising the factories and planting new sisal plants. Although, there were some delays in implementation and financing, the initial results were nevertheless promising.

The tea factories were modernised, and 2,500 hectares of new sisal was planted and major improvements made to the basic infrastructure such as housing, workers' welfare, water and electricity supply and roads. The workers' morale was high

Toyota main office, Dar es Salaam late 1990s.

and there were fewer labour shortages. Despite these successes, some of the basic assumptions underlying the revitalisation programme proved too ambitious especially in relation to the production of tea and profitability from exports.

When the CDC loan was drawn down in 1990, the world market price of tea was about USD 3.00 a kilo. When the loan grace period of three years was over and the loan repayment was to commence, the price of tea had dropped by 80 percent to USD 0.60 per kilo. It takes seven to ten years for new-planted sisal to reach maturity. As old sisal fields are planted with new sisal, it naturally follows that production will fall by at least 10 percent every year for seven to ten years until it begins to increase again. The company had estimated that positive revenue from tea would fund sisal deficits. When world market prices of tea collapsed in 1993 this didn't happen.

There were many other causes for the looming liquidity crisis. Despite the economic adjustment programmes, the Tanzanian shilling was not devalued, but remained artificially strong, hence decreasing revenues from agricultural exports. As a result of the economic adjustment policy, domestic inflation was high and all major production costs, like wages, electricity, and fuel, were higher than estimated. Furthermore, desperate to find revenues to pay for its expenditure, the government was constantly increasing all forms of direct and indirect taxation. The company calculated that it was paying thirty different kinds of taxes in 1995. The Price Waterhouse Associates' Report proved to be too optimistic.

A last ditch effort was made in 1995 by Karimjee Agriculture to reschedule the loans and convert outstanding loans and interest into equity. CDC readily agreed to a rescue plan but CRDB, being a quasi-governmental bank, was bureaucratic and unwilling to be cooperative. New investments were needed and Karimjee Agriculture estimated that it would need an additional six million USD and that returns would only materialise after twelve years assuming that no new taxes would be imposed. In the meantime Hatim had made an appeal to the President but by the time a response was received it was too little and too late.

In 1994 Toyota Japan informed the family that they should consider selling IML to Lonrho. (The name of International Motor Mart was streamlined to International Motors Limited, 'IML', in 1991). Toyota was concerned that Karimjees had run out of funds to invest in IML as a result of the worsening situation at Karimjee Jivanjee Estates. Lonrho was a UK based company famous for its charismatic leader Tiny Rowland and was active in many business ventures in Africa. Lonrho was already a Toyota distributor in Kenya, Uganda, Zambia, Malawi and Zimbabwe. The Karimjees became interested in this option as a way of raising capital, firstly for shareholder benefit and secondly, to prop up Karimjee Agriculture. After one year of talks, the negotiations with Lonrho fell through, as the two parties could neither agree on the price nor on many other thorny issues.

The collapse of the sale of IML to Lonrho sealed the fate of Karimjee Agriculture. After 75 years (1921 - 1996) Karimjee's daring and often very profitable investment in tea and sisal had come to an end. In January 1996, the Karimjees called in their 'secured' creditors CDC and CRDB and informed them that they would surrender the company with all the plantations and assets to them on 1 April 1996. CDC and CRDB appointed Coopers & Lybrand as receivers to sell all the estates to recover their debts. Whilst regretting the outcome, Hatim Karimjee took responsibility and said "This tragedy happened on my watch and so I must take the primary responsibility". He was the first Karimjee director in six generations to give up a major Karimjee company. Hatim offered his resignation to the Board of Directors but the chairman, Hakim Adamjee, did not accept it because he felt that the entire Board should share the responsibility.

Sentiment was running very high among the family in

1996 as everyone recognised that the agricultural business was an essential part of the reputation of the family. Many felt humiliated by this defeat. However some pragmatic members of the family pointed out that Toyota was making good profits and now that the family was out of the agricultural business, family members could benefit from those profits. Around this time it was also decided that the business would be managed through regular meetings of the Board of Directors reporting annually to a shareholders General Meeting. It was agreed that management would report to the Directors, and that the Directors would keep the family (shareholders) fully informed about the managerial and financial status of the business. In conjunction with this, a number of younger members of the family joined the board as non-executive directors.

In short, the Karimjee family went through some turbulent decades in this chapter. Tanganyika became Tanzania and the family played an important role in the transition to independence. Abdulakarim supported the education of many African politicians to be. He presided over the independence ceremony in 1961. The Karimjee family critically supported their President. However, most of the Karimjees could not bear his nationalisation politics. They left the country for economic reasons, but also to take the responsibility for their children's education. The Karimjees lost most of their real estate properties, but remained in business with their agricultural and Toyota businesses. They went through a very rough period during the crackdown and the economic decline in the 1980s. Eventually, they lost their agricultural business. Despite the economic, social and personal losses, some of the family members were always willing to keep up the good name of the Karimjees. Eventually they had to sacrifice the agricultural business, but after hard work and new investments the Toyota franchise remained the profitable cash cow for the family.

Despite these turbulent years, perhaps because of it, the Karimjees remained faithful to their religious and charitable responsibilities. This is another important element of the Karimjee Jivanjee family. In the almost 200 years of history they are still seen as Bohra Muslims and their charitable contributions have reached far beyond their own community. They are still very much attached to East Africa. The importance of religion and charities in the Karimjee Jivanjee history will be described in the next chapter.

CHAPTER 5 · POLITICAL TURMOIL AND ECONOMIC DECLINE 1964 - 1990

126

CHAPTER 6

Religion, Politics and Charity 1880 - 2004

Religion affects all aspects of life, as it can be related to food habits, dress habits, marriage patterns, inheritance, practices and conventions surrounding birth and death and many other aspects of life. Religion has played an undeniable role in the Karimjee family, the Karimjee businesses and the Karimjee charities, since charity and good deeds is one of the five pillars of Islam. In this chapter a few of the major donations of the Karimjee family are described, most notably that of Karimjee Hall, the 'most splendid gift of all' according to a local paper.[44]

Moreover, some Karimjees donated their time and capabilities in public work, most notably Tayabali Karimjee, Abdulkarim Karimjee and Yusufali Karimjee. From this perspective it is clear that there were strong interrelationships, or even symbiotic relationships, between the religious aspects of life, charities, and political ambitions and the role as a business family. In short, this chapter is about these symbiotic relationships and how the Karimjee family members served the East African community. This chapter starts from a historical perspective by describing the origins of Islam and the Dawoodi Bohra community.

The message of Islam reached India through trade, war and conquest somewhere between the 8th and 12th centuries. The Hindu rulers, however, were very ambivalent towards the Muslim invaders from the West, who were mainly seen as conquerors, but at the same time Arab merchants supplied them with goods and scientific and regional knowledge, as well as sharing their experiences. Eventually, the (Muslim) Sufi movement of the 8th and 9th centuries became very successful in converting

Karimjee Hall became the TZS 1000 nomination of the stamps series: Old buildings and architecture in Tanzania.

various Hindu communities in Northern India. Even today, the Dawoodi Bohras claim a Brahmin origin, whereas other Muslim communities like the Khoja Ismailis and Ithnasheries contend that they were originally Lohanas (or Kshatryia).[45]

This type of community-wise conversion has led to a religious and cultural mix, which makes it difficult to identify either Hindu or Muslim roots. Obviously the converts accepted the five pillars of Islam, i.e. the avowal of faith: "There is no God but Allah and Mohammed is His Prophet", prayers are said five times a day, celebrate Ramadan, Hajj, charity or good deeds. In addition, the Muslim faith plays an important role in all matters concerning marriage, divorce, inheritance and so on. Many rituals, however, relate to South Asian culture as well, rather than religion. The use of a coconut in purification rituals as well as shaving the head of a newborn, for example, is seen in both Hindu and Muslim traditions.

The Dawoodi Bohras are known as a close-knit, self-contained community in all respects, not just in religious affairs. After they arrived in East Africa they were quick to set up their own *masjids* (mosques), schools, and charity organisations. The local Bohra business communities often funded these institutions, which in return helped to establish local religious business communities. Other Muslim communities used the

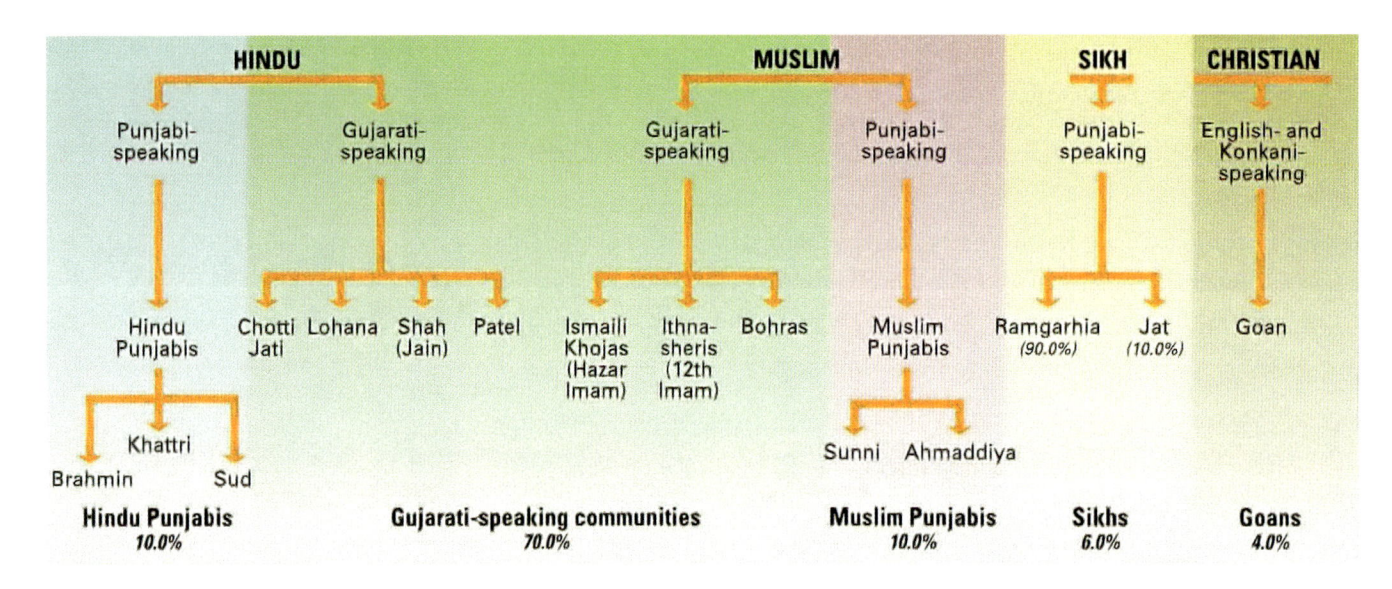

TABLE 5 ASIAN SUB-GROUPINGS IN EAST AFRICA BY RELIGION, LANGUAGE AND CASTE

HINDU		MUSLIM		SIKH	CHRISTIAN
Punjabi-speaking	Gujarati-speaking	Gujarati-speaking	Punjabi-speaking	Punjabi-speaking	English- and Konkani-speaking
Hindu Punjabis	Chotti Jati, Lohana, Shah (Jain), Patel	Ismaili Khojas (Hazar Imam), Ithna-sheris (12th Imam), Bohras	Muslim Punjabis → Sunni, Ahmaddiya	Ramgarhia (90.0%), Jat (10.0%)	Goan
Khattri → Brahmin, Sud					
Hindu Punjabis 10.0%	**Gujarati-speaking communities 70.0%**		**Muslim Punjabis 10.0%**	**Sikhs 6.0%**	**Goans 4.0%**

Source: Brij Lal (ed), *The Encyclopedia of the Indian Diaspora,* Singapore 2006, p. 260.

same strategies as well, like the Ismailis and the Ithnasheries. As in other Muslim communities, the Bohra *masjids* are mostly designed for men and women equally. Women usually do not visit the *masjid* for daily prayers, but they are very active during religious festivals. They are often responsible for the social affairs and for preparing the food. During festivals and on many other occasions, men and women share their communal meals in the *masjid*. Within the Bohra community, the *masjid* not only has a religious function but is also used for other ceremonies, like naming ceremonies and marriages. One of the more important ceremonies is that of *misaq*, or the formal initiation into the community at puberty. It often takes the form of a sacred oath taken in front of the Imam.

Everyone has the need to care for others. Caring for children, spouses and immediate relatives is a basic instinct. The first step in 'charity and philanthropy' is to go beyond the boundaries of immediate family and loved ones. Eventually, this means surpassing the extended family or one's self-defined 'community'. The second step is acceptance of a certain degree of self-sacrifice whilst not expecting anything in return for the charitable contributions and voluntary work, not even respect or social prestige. The final step is to allow all communities, races or nationalities to have access to the charity. This amounts to humanism in its purest and truest form. In this section we will see that the Karimjee family reached this final step at an early stage.

Three factors inspired the charitable contributions of the Karimjees: (1) The experience of being migrants and depending on other community members may have encouraged the Karimjees to serve others; (2) A part of their charitable contributions was definitely inspired by religion; (3) Lastly, the political ambitions of Karimjee family members may have been motivated by business interests, but more often the Karimjees served the interests of the wider business communities as well.

Most new South Asian migrants in East Africa depended on the goodwill of other migrants (mostly family and community members) in East Africa in the late 19th century. They had left their friends and relatives in India behind, they may have borrowed money for the voyage or spent their last savings only to arrive almost penniless in East Africa. Many did not speak English, Arabic or Swahili. They were not accustomed to the local rules and bureaucratic system so it was almost impossible to acquire a trading license, some credit or even a small mattress to sleep on. Even among Asians, they were often strangers outside their own communities.

We know that during the first weeks or months after arrival, many migrants stayed with relatives and friends or in community houses. These houses were informally organised, often on the premises of a South Asian trader who had already become established in East Africa. In many cities, stories are told that after a dhow arrived from India, people were immediately directed to the house of a certain trader where they could spend the first couple of nights. Within these first weeks or months they were helped to find a job, to start a small business and find a more permanent place to stay. Many migrant families did not forget what it had been like to be poor themselves. These migrant experiences may have paved the way for many successful Asian traders and businessmen to enter the field of charity.[46] In the case of the Karimjee family we have seen how Karimjee Jivanjee came back from India empty-handed, because he had lost his cargo. Despite this, he was able – with the help of community members – to build up his trading empire.

Religion was another source for the development of charitable organisations within the South Asian community. Many Muslim communities follow a 'rule of thumb', giving five to ten percent of their income or time to charities. Often this is divided between *sadaqah*, or 'voluntary and personal charity' and *zakat*, the religious idea that wealth must be shared with others. Within the Bohra community, a part of this was formalised, because the religious functions and services required all kinds of taxes to be levied on their followers. Interestingly, one of the pre-conditions of Bohra charities is the idea of 'helping people to help themselves'. Thus, they prefer to invest their money in founding schools, and other long-term sustainable investments, rather than to participate in sporadic alms giving. Consequently, one rarely sees beggars outside the Bohra Mosque.[47] Even today, education plays an important part in the Karimjee charities (from building schools to the awarding scholarships).

The spiritual leader of the Bohras visited his community in East Africa in 1968. The government of Tanganyika became seriously concerned when it heard that large amounts of money were being collected as religious taxes and gifts and were being exchanged for gold in order to transfer the funds to Bombay. This went against the existing foreign exchange regulations. The government reacted on 14 August 1968 by exiling His Holiness Seyedna from Tanzania. The Karimjee family were blamed for this grave embarrassment and were excommunicated from the community by their spiritual leaders. They argued that Abdulkarim, being a very influential figure, must have been responsible for the expulsion. They thought that even if he was not responsible, he should have done something to prevent the expulsion. Abdulkarim as a pious God-fearing Muslim was deeply upset by the expulsion of his religious leader, and very offended that he was being blamed for something that he had not done and had no control over. Nevertheless, he tried to remain calm and mild in tone in his subsequent correspondence.

The political ambitions of South Asians in East Africa were often a direct response to anti-Indian legislation, and to the speeches and attitudes of European arrivals in East Africa. Most Europeans did not realise that many South Asians had

Yusufali Karimjee and Tayabali Karimjee were invited to join a lunch in the honour of A.M. Jeevanjee in London in 1910.

Seated back (left to right); Mr George Pollock, Mr N.M. Cooper, Mr A.S.M. Anik, Sir M.M. Bhownaree, Mr Ratan Tata, Sir George McKenzie, Rt. Hon. Syeed Ameer Ali, A.M. Jeevanjee, Sir J. Dunlop Smith, Sir George Birdwood, Mr Mirza, A.A. Brig, Mr C.A. Latif, Mr F. H. Brown, Mr Moos, Mr Long.

Seated front (left to right); Mr Leo Wheintal (representative), Mr Hajee Ahmed Devji, Dr Kaka, Mr Frank Birdwood, Mr L.W. Ritch, Dr Abdul Majid, Mr Fazulbhoy Visram, Makor Atkins, Mr Austin Low, Mr M.T. Kaderbhoy, Mr Nicholson, Mr Yusufali Karimjee, Mr R.D. Galbraith, Mr Tayebali Alibhoy Karimjee, Mr Lynch, Dr Kapadia, Mr Adamali Yusufali, Mr W. Coldstream, Mr Auerbach.

arrived in East Africa long before the Europeans. Eventually, the Indian Association was founded in Mombasa as early as 1900 to institutionalise and collect the grievances of the Asian community and to give them a voice. The founder of the Association was L.M. Savle, who was supported by the wealthiest and most influential Indians in East Africa at that time: Alidina Visram, and the brothers A.M. and T.M. Jeevanjee. The Indian Association would be instrumental in defending the political and economic interests of Asians in East Africa. Their first big issue was to protest against European exclusiveness in the highlands of Kenya. The Association generally used the liberal argument of equal rights, i.e. equal representation and equal shares. In doing so, they defended their own interests, but sometimes that of Africans as well. The Association also helped to improve the education, healthcare and welfare of the South Asians in East Africa by negotiating politically favourable conditions for building mosques, schools and hospitals in the area.

It was in this political arena that the first supporting activities of the Karimjee Jivanjee family were recorded.[48] In the 1900s and 1910s, Zanzibar Asians felt the changes caused by the growing political control of the British, in particular, the increase in custom duties (by more than 50%) as well as the growing British colonial bureaucracy, which annoyed the Asians. In addition, privileges like holding religious processions without permits were abolished. In September 1909, there was a mass meeting in Zanzibar Town organised by the newly-formed political organisation: the Committee of Indians, under the presidency of Yusufali Karimjee. During the meeting, a memorandum was approved, expressing the 'dissatisfaction with certain laws passed since 1908 which limited their liberty and injuriously affected their commercial interests'.[49]

In Mombasa another leader of the business community, A.M. Jeevanjee, had presented a list of similar grievances to the colonial government. He was eventually invited to present his case in London. He decided that it was better not to go alone and invited several respected members of business communities in East Africa as well as India to accompany him. These included Yusufali Karimjee and Tayabali Karimjee

In 1914, the Committee of Indians was reorganised and became the Indian National Association of Zanzibar. A cousin of Yusufali Karimjee, Yusufali Esmailjee Jivanjee, followed in his footsteps by presenting the 'Memorandum on the Report of the Commission on Agriculture' in 1923. He was a member of the Zanzibar Protectorate Council. In that position he firmly criticised the government's position that Indians were responsible for the Indebtedness of Agriculturalists (read Arabs and Swahili) on Zanzibar. In addition, he passed judgment on the method of collecting the clove duty, which was especially to the disadvantage of Asian clove producers.[50]

Grievances about government legislation and the high taxes – compared to what British and other European traders paid – continued in the 1920s and 1930s. The newspapers of that period reveal that Yusufali Karimjee was the major spokesman

Yusufali Karimjee was known as "the lion of Zanzibar" for his bold and straightforward political opinions. Tanganyika Herald, 15th December 1934.

of the Indian business community (Hindus and Muslims) in Zanzibar. He was called 'the leader of the public opinion created in Zanzibar against anti-Indian measures' or 'The Lion of Zanzibar'. The headline of one article in the Tanganyika Herald was: 'The Lion of Zanzibar Roars'.[51] And roar he did, but with rational and straightforward rhetoric.

Some examples: Often the British argued that they had to look after the welfare of the Africans, but Yusufali always demonstrated that Indians in Zanzibar were not against any legislation in favour of Arabs and natives, but that they were against the government's policy of protecting one section of the Zanzibari community *at the expense* of another. When the British argued that they had reduced import duties for fresh butter and milk, ghee and cigarettes, Karimjee demonstrated that the Europeans used milk to feed their children, not the natives! In the case of ghee, only the middle and upper classes of the Indian population profited from the reductions, because they used ghee, but not the poorer sections of the community. In the case of cigarettes, Karimjee shows that a native – who only smokes two or three cigarettes a day – does not profit from a tax reduction of 'eight to nine' annas after every *thousand* cigarettes, but rather the Europeans who smoke cigarettes by the hundreds and buy in thousands. And then Karimjee added: "If His Excellency wishes to really benefit the poor natives, we want the duty on rice and kangas to be reduced! These are their real necessities. Then alone can we say that the Government is doing something for the natives."[52] After a handful of examples, where Yusufali showed that the government legislation was to the disadvantage of the Indian trading community in Zanzibar, he concluded, "the policy of the Government underlying this movement is to rob Indian Peter to pay British Paul."

During the early 1930s, the colonial government policies tended to focus on the most important trade and industries of the island, i.e. cloves. The government's key concern was twofold. On the one hand, it wanted to protect Arabs from having to mortgage their land to Indian traders, and on the other hand it wished to increase the tax revenue. The Indian National Association, however, argued that most of the measures taken by the government would crush Indian retailers, deprive the Indians of money legitimately invested in trade and mortgages, and ultimately undermine all commercial activities. They therefore forced the Indians to leave the country. The Government of India appointed K.P.S. Menon, a former agent in Ceylon, to look into the matter. He blankly concluded that most decrees were "calculated to cause irretrievable damage to Indian interests and will practically oust the Indian trader from Zanzibar". Despite these conclusions, the report did not have the desired effect and the Colonial Office bluntly dismissed it as "useless".[52] Yusufali often used the same line of argument, keenly estimating the weight of his position. In a speech published in the Tanganyika Herald, he posed the often-cited rhetorical question:

"One would like to know what would be the duration of residency for members of any particular race to acquire the same rights as those enjoyed by the indigenous population. For, be it remembered, according to historical evidence, Indians have been settled in East Africa for pretty nearly 400 years." [54]

The Karimjees slowly became public figures because of their political opinions and growing involvement in charities. Donating mainly through three family trusts, in Zanzibar in the 1920s the Karimjee companies began giving five percent of their profits to charity in the good years and at least three per cent in the bad.[55] In accordance with their philosophy 'of helping to help themselves' an important part of their charitable funding was put into scholarships and schools. In addition, they also donated to religious charities and charities concerned with medical service and hospitals.

One of the early examples of a public charity act was the marriage of Abdulla Currimjee Moriswalla with Husseinabai Yusufali Karimjee and Abdulkarim Karimjee and Batul Noorbhai. Both were married on the same day on 8 May 1930. On this occasion, the proud father of the groom, Yusufali, announced the construction of an Asian Maternity Home in Zanzibar for the Bohra community. It was to be named after their mother and grandmother, Fatemabai. On that same day, Tayabali Karimjee expressed his desire to donate Rs 50,000 in memory of his father, Hassanali Karimjee, to build a hospital in his name. In addition, a number of smaller charities were announced. The Tanganyika Opinion stated: "The Karimjee House is also well-known for their former charities in Bombay, and elsewhere, especially the one of Rs 275,000 for building the Bohra guesthouse in Bombay in 1929 and a recent one of Rs 35,000 for completing a Bohra school in Karachi." [56]

Three main charity trusts along the family lines were established in 1940. First, there was the Mohamedali A. Karimjee Jivanjee Trust, which built schools, mosques and an African community centre. It also contributed to the King George VI Memorial Library in Tanga and towards educational maintenance in Zanzibar. In 1958, the total sum of donations amounted to £85,000. Second, there was the Sir Yusufali Charitable Trust, which has specialised in higher education scholarships for East African students. In general, half the students went to Britain, whereas the other half went to India, Pakistan and East Africa. It also contributed to the building of educational organisations and institutes. In 1958, the total amount spent on charities was £200,000. Third, Sir Tayabali Karimjee established two trusts in the names of both his parents. He donated more than £350,000 to hospitals, schools, halls, clinics and clubs.[57]

The historian Robert Gregory summarised the total amount of the charities of Sir Tayabali Karimjee in East Africa as follows: "By 1963 Seth Tayabali Hassanali A. Karimjee, chairman of the Karimjee group of Companies, Zanzibar, had endowed the following institutions."

TABLE 6 LIST OF CHARITIES AND THEIR VALUES

Hassanali Karimjee General Hospital, Zanzibar	£	67,500
Karimjee Hall, Dar es Salaam	£	40,000
Muslims Girl's School, Zanzibar	£	26,000
Bohra School Mombasa	£	25,000
Bohra Maternity Home, Dar es Salaam	£	22,500
Bohra Maternity Home, Mombasa	£	20,000
Bohra Jamnatkhana and Marriage Hall, Tanga	£	15,000
Bohra Nursery School, Dar es Salaam	£	12,500
Sports Stadium Zanzibar	£	10,000
Nursery School, Tanga	£	10,000
Sports Gymkhana Tanga	£	7,500
Total	£	256,000
Valued in 2009	£	4.700,000 [58]

Source: Robert G. Gregory, *The Rise and Fall of Philanthropy in East Africa. The Asian Contribution*, Transaction Publishers, London, 1992, p. 50.

The Yusufali Karimjee Charitable Trust was the main donor of the Tanzania National Library with a sum of £65,000. The fund also contributed substantially to the Faculty of Arts of the University of Dar es Salaam. Sir Yusufali Karimjee eventually left one third of his money to charity, in line with his motto "wealth imposes obligations". He spent more than £150,000 on mosques, schools, hospitals and the like. Probably the greatest charitable contribution of the Karimjee Jivanjee family was the white neo-classical edifice, Karimjee Hall, which was handed over to the Dar es Salaam City Council in 1955. It was meant as a community hall for the city council. But the city council soon rented it out to be used as the colonial Legislative Council and later, after independence was declared, as the House of Parliament.

KARIMJEE HALL: THE MOST SPLENDID GIFT OF ALL

Whatever the importance of the charities of various Karimjee foundations, by far the most impressive, and most important gift, was that of the Karimjee Hall. The hall was originally given as a community hall to the new municipal council of Dar es Salaam, but it soon served as the municipal council itself and later as Legislative Council. Currently it houses the Office of the Mayor of Dar es salaam, the City Council Meeting Chamber and also serves as a hall for public functions.

The Karimjee Hall was an exceptional charity because funding was provided by all the many different Trusts of the family Mohamedali Trust, Hassanali Trust, Yusufali Trust as well as through donations from the Karimjee Group of Companies. Therefore the four historical champions of the family signed the donor certificate: Sir Yusufali Karimjee, Sir Tayabali Karimjee, Abdulla Karimjee and Abdulkarim Karimjee. Together they represented the Karimjee Jivanjee & Co. Ltd., the International Motor Mart Ltd., Karimjee Jivanjee Estates Ltd., and Karimjee Properties Ltd. This is a clear indication that whatever differences there were between family members in respect of business issues or at the personal level; they were perfectly able to overcome these matters for the benefit of the family, community and country as a whole.

Second, the gift was meant "for the use, benefit and enjoyment of all people and races and creeds who do dwell within the municipality of Dar es Salaam". In his opening speech, Yusufali Karimjee, the oldest family member at that time, wished and prayed that:

> " (…) the hall will prove its utility to Dar es Salaam in bringing together its citizens, and that the meetings and deliberations which will take place under its roof will contribute materially to the general well being, peace, progress and prosperity of everyone living in the progressive territory of Tanganyika." [59]

The original idea of the Hall goes back to 1949. India had just gained its independence and it was conceivable that the East African countries would achieve their own independence. The family wished to donate a community hall to the city council of Dar es Salaam. At that time, the total costs of the project were estimated at £ 15,000. However, there had been many delays, and in 1953 the total costs were estimated in various papers at between £ 35,000 and £ 50,000. Mr J. Goldthorp was the architect of the building. It incorporated the Municipal Council with a Council Chamber suite in keeping with the importance of Dar es Salaam as the capital of Tanganyika. Later, the hall also provided accommodation for the Legislative Council, until a more permanent chamber was built. The chamber could seat 30 councillors, which exceeded the requirements of the day.

The building included a public gallery in the Council Chamber which accommodated 60 people. The Main Assembly Hall's design included ionic columns and a panel motif to impart the sense of spaciousness and dignity befitting a public hall.

From left to the right: Abid Karimjee, Lady Twining, Lady Banoo Jivanjee, His Excellency Sir Edward Twining; Sir Yusufali Karimjee, Abdulla M.A. Karimjee OBE

CHAPTER 6 · RELIGION, POLITICS AND CHARITY: SERVING THE EAST AFRICAN COMMUNITY 1880 - 2004

Sir Edward Twining, the Governor of Tanganyika opened the Karimjee Hall on 16 April 1955. There was a huge garden party with more than 700 guests, including his wife Lady Twining, Sir Herbert Cox (Chief Secretary) and Mr R de S. Stapledon, the Speaker of the Legislative Council. There were also international guests, like the Mayor of Nairobi, R.S. Alexander, and the Town Clerk, Mr John Riseborough. The press wrote that this was the 'most memorable date in the history of the Municipal Council of Dar es Salaam'.

MUNICIPAL COUNCIL OF DAR ES SALAAM

At a Special Meeting of the Municipal Council of Dar es Salaam held in the Council Chamber at the Karimjee Hall in the Municipality of Dar es Salaam on the 16th April, 1955

IT WAS RESOLVED

That this Council does hereby accept the gift of the Karimjee Hall, so generously offered by the Karimjee Family, for the use benefit and enjoyment of the people of Dar es Salaam and places on record its gratitude to the said Family for their munificence and public spirit in presenting such a magnificent gift.

In witness whereof the Common Seal of the Municipal Council of Dar es Salaam was hereunto affixed in the presence of :—

MAYOR

TOWN CLERK

KNOW ALL MEN BY THESE PRESENTS THAT

WHEREAS the Karimjee Family came to the shores of Azania one hundred and thirty years ago as traders and merchant adventurers from India, and being well received and kindly treated, founded and established their house in Zanzibar and on the Azania Coast Lands; and

WHEREAS the House of Karimjee, by the Grace of God, prospered and took great part in the enterprise of developing these lands and opening the way for trade, commerce and agriculture, and being desirous of ensuring that a measure of the fruits of their industry and endeavour shall be devoted to the well being of the people of the country in which their House is established and which they have come to love in loyalty as their own;

NOW THEREFOR the members of the House of Karimjee, having caused this building to be erected as a token of their deep and loyal affection for this Territory and its peoples, do hereby give, donate and convey the said building, which shall be known as KARIMJEE HALL, to the Municipal Council of Dar es Salaam and dedicate it in perpetuity for the use benefit and enjoyment of all people of all races and creeds who dwell within the Municipality of Dar es Salaam.

Given under the hand of

[signature]
YUSUFALI ALIBHAI KARIMJEE JIVANJEE

[signature]
TAYABALI HASANALI ALIBHAI KARIMJEE

[signature]
ABDULLA MOHAMEDALI ALIBHAI KARIMJEE

[signature]
ABDULKARIM YUSUFALI ALIBHAI KARIMJEE

On behalf of the members of the House of Karimjee.

This sixteenth day of April, 1955 at Dar es Salaam.

PORTRAIT

TAYABALI KARIMJEE 1897 - 1987

Tayabali Karimjee was born in 1897 in Zanzibar, where he went to primary school. His life revolved around three things: the family business, politics and charities. He travelled a lot to Europe, South Asia (Karachi) and Egypt. In 1930 he gave away 60 percent of his earnings to charities in East Africa in general and Zanzibar in particular. He was knighted in 1955 for his public and charitable contributions to the East African community. During his life he became close friends with the Sultan of Zanzibar and other important people in the history of Zanzibar. During the Zanzibar Revolution (1964) his house was taken over by the new government. After the revolution, he became active in service organisations such as Rotary and Freemasonry in Karachi. The last years of his life were spent in Karachi, but he constantly longed for Zanzibar. In short, his life was a dynamic one.

Tayabali was the only son of Hassanali Karimjee Jivanjee (1872 - 1918). Like his father, he was brought into the family business at an early age. During his childhood, his father Hassanali and his uncles Mohamedali and Yusufali ran the business. They lived in the Hurumzi family house in Zanzibar, where the family stayed together at that time. Tayabali was very fond of Sugra, the daughter of his uncle Mohamedali. They played together from an early age. It was known that they had been exchanging love letters while they were in their teens. Eventually it was decided that the two were destined for each other and they married at an early age. The death of his older sister Sukan (1911), who was still quite young, as well as his father's death (1918), left Tayabali (then aged 21) with just his mother Zenam. His uncle Mohamedali took him under his wing and taught him the ins and outs of the Karimjee Jivanjee & Co. business in Zanzibar.

Tayabali soon became the youngest member in the Karimjee business. Being the only son he inherited all the shares held by his father. Thus, he ended up with approximately the same number of shares as his uncles (33 per cent), while he was 20 years younger than Mohamedali and Yusufali. In other words, he owned the same stake in the company as his old uncles, but he was far less experienced. In addition, it soon became clear that

This picture was taken around 1900 in Karachi. At the top left we see Yusufali Nurbhai Jafferjee, he was the father of Batul, who became the wife of Abdulkarim. Next to him is Ghulamhussein N. Jafferjee, the father of Zohra, who became the wife of Abdulkader. The small boy in the middle is Tayabali.

Tayabali dressed up complete with his decorations, probably in the 1930s.

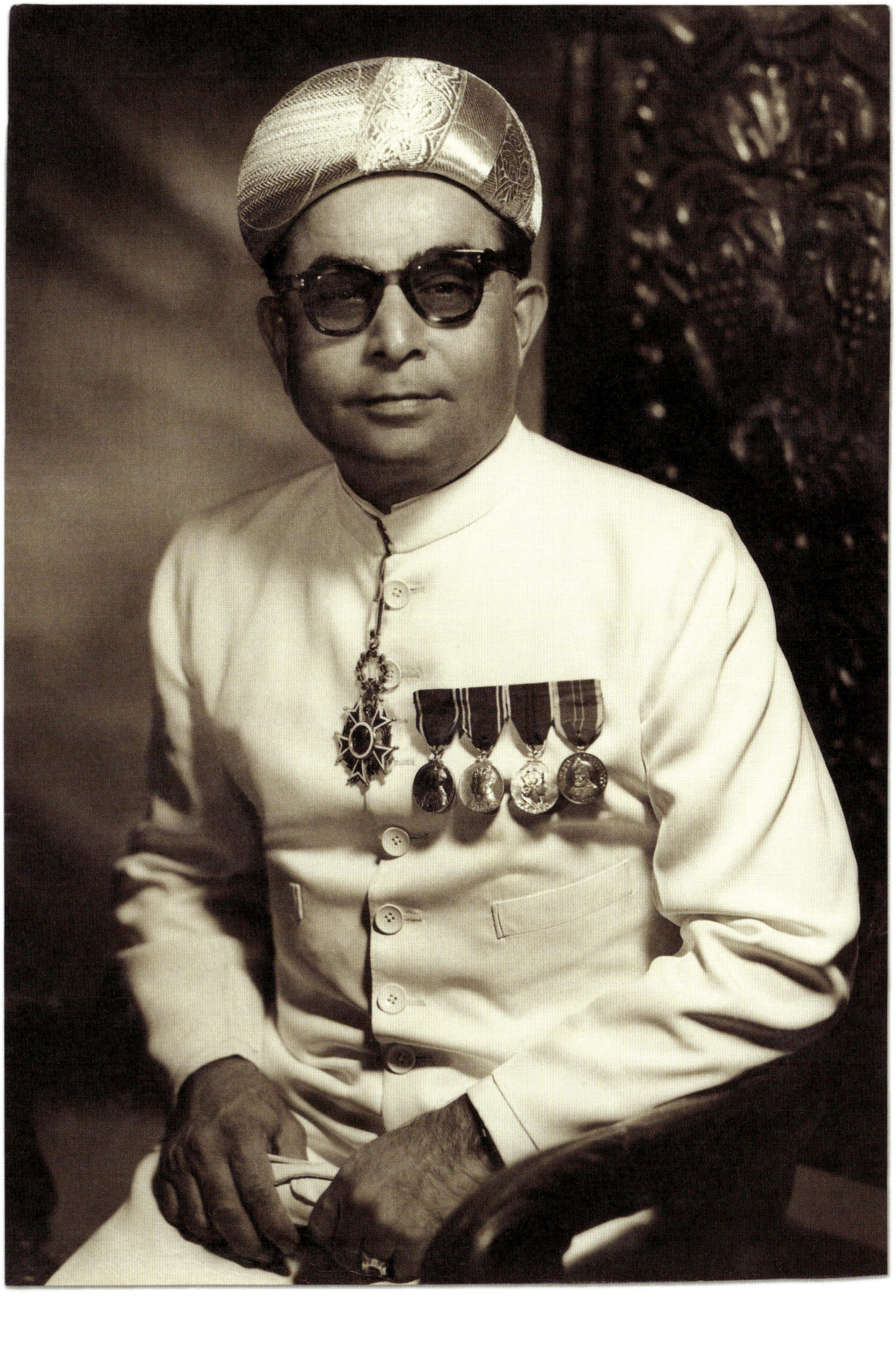

On the Historic Day of 15th July, 1937
— Zanzibarians Observe Hartal —

(1), (2), (3) Important Main Business Centres
(4) One Indian Retail Shop kept open under Police Protection
(5) Mammoth Mass Meeting on Saxi's Ground
(6) Hon'ble Taibali addressing
(7) A Procession with Hon. Taiab after he walked out of Le[gislature]

CHAPTER 6 · RELIGION, POLITICS AND CHARITY 1880 - 2004

A small compilation of an historic event taken from a family album.
Tayabali walked out of the Legislative Council on 15 July 1937.
He was carried shoulder-high and all Indian shops were closed that day.

his uncles had produced a large number of offspring. This would eventually lead to a dilution of their share in the family business. Nevertheless, like in many South Asian business families, the numbers are a small part of the balance in authority and influence in the family. More importance is generally attached to the notion of 'seniority'. Tayabali became the head of the family in Zanzibar after his uncle Mohammedali passed away in 1940.

Tayabali was known as a very strict and Victorian-minded person. He believed in firm rules and discipline. He was the oldest of the cousins, and felt responsible for disciplining the youngsters. Some of the youngsters in the family saw him as a kind of 'Godfather' of the family. However, at the same time he was a warm-hearted and loving husband. Whenever he had time he enjoyed his family life at home.

He admired the efficiency of the British colonial government in the Raj as well as East Africa. He travelled to Europe in 1910, at the age of 13, together with his uncle Yusufali. He could easily switch from a British suit to a Bohra dress and turban. He was also able to communicate with people from various backgrounds. In addition, he had a knack for smoothing family relations as well as mediating in complicated business arrangements.

The First World War changed the colonial equilibrium dramatically. German, British and Indian traders who had previously traded their (agricultural) products and provided trading services to each other – albeit often in a racially organised environment – now became war enemies. Very little is known about this period and its direct aftermath. Tayabali was an experienced traveller, and Karachi – the birthplace of his mother – was one of his favourite destinations. It is likely that he spent a considerable amount of his time there. The fact is that there are hardly any records relating to Tayabali's life for the period between 1914 - 1930. There are some minor references saying that Tayabali took some interest in educational affairs in Zanzibar in the 1910s. He soon developed a great interest in sports and the scouting movement. He was especially fond of polo and cricket. Later he started to organise cricket tournaments for East Africans. The Karimjee Jivanjee family eventually supported this

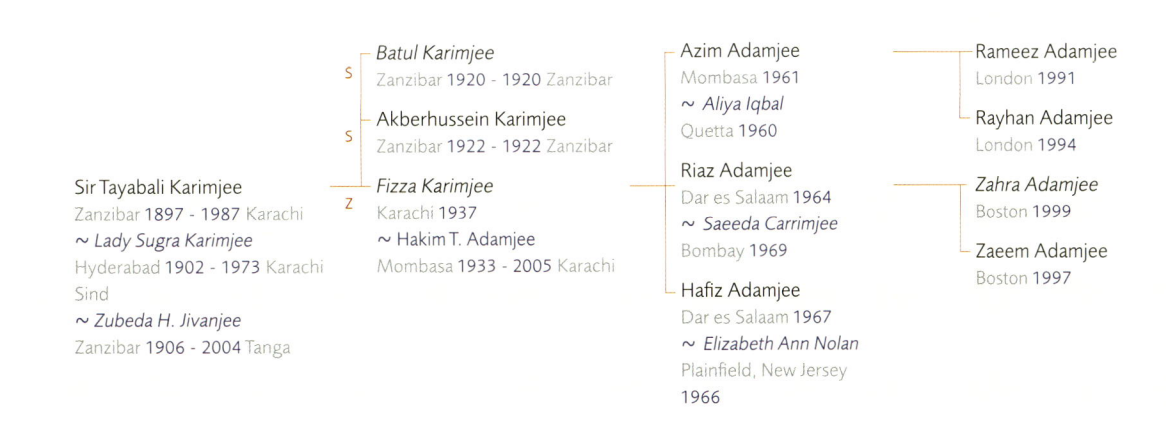

| 141

Sir Tayabali Karimjee
Zanzibar 1897 - 1987 Karachi
~ Lady Sugra Karimjee
Hyderabad 1902 - 1973 Karachi
Sind
~ Zubeda H. Jivanjee
Zanzibar 1906 - 2004 Tanga

S ┌ Batul Karimjee
  │ Zanzibar 1920 - 1920 Zanzibar
S ├ Akberhussein Karimjee
  │ Zanzibar 1922 - 1922 Zanzibar
Z └ Fizza Karimjee
    Karachi 1937
    ~ Hakim T. Adamjee
    Mombasa 1933 - 2005 Karachi

Azim Adamjee
Mombasa 1961
~ Aliya Iqbal
Quetta 1960

Riaz Adamjee
Dar es Salaam 1964
~ Saeeda Carrimjee
Bombay 1969

Hafiz Adamjee
Dar es Salaam 1967
~ Elizabeth Ann Nolan
Plainfield, New Jersey
1966

┌ Rameez Adamjee
│ London 1991
├ Rayhan Adamjee
│ London 1994
├ Zahra Adamjee
│ Boston 1999
└ Zaeem Adamjee
  Boston 1997

as they sponsored what came to be known as the prestigious Tayabali Karimjee Cricket Cup. The Zanzibar Scout Club had a great well-wisher in Tayabali Karimjee.

Later he became interested in public office. He was elected president of the Indian Association in 1930 for a two-year term.

Tayabali and his wife Sugra.

In that office he tried to serve the Indian community and the larger interests of the Protectorate. In 1932 His Highness the Sultan was pleased to nominate him as an unofficial member of the Legislative Council. Tayabali continued to be a member for twelve years. He eventually wrote himself into Zanzibari business history by walking out after the Legislative Council passed the Clove Monopoly Bill on 23 July 1937. He realised that this bill was beneficial for the Europeans in Zanzibar, but not for the Zanzibaris themselves. The bill was a direct insult to emerging Arab-Asian relations in Zanzibar because its hidden aim was to separate financiers (the Asians) from the landowners (the Arabs) in order to politically control both groups separately. Moreover, the Zanzibari people were likely to be the hardest hit, because of the decreasing profits derived from the clove trade. All of the more than 200 Indian spectators stood up and applauded as Tayabali rose from his chair. They followed him in procession and carried him shoulder-high. On the same day, all shops were closed immediately. Before noon, the English Bazaar ceased trading. Everyone on the Zanzibar streets seemed to be mourning, as people in different groups wept and poured out their hearts. On the same day, at four o'clock, a mass meeting was held, chaired by Tayabali. Eventually, the Indians in Zanzibar successfully filed a petition with the Government of India, in order to pressure the Legislative Council in Zanzibar into changing the conditions of the trade.

Tayabali liked to travel, if not for business then for pleasure. In 1932 he went to Egypt with Abdulla, Abdulla's daughter Zehra and Kianga. They went to see the pyramids, went on a safari along the Nile and visited Cairo. In 1934, he visited Ahmedabad (in India) to meet with Mr Jeewanjee Currimjee Morriswalla (the CJs from Mauritius). He learnt that there was a flying club in Ahmedabad and he met the secretary of the club. He became a member and arranged a flight to Karachi via Rajkot and Jamnagar – two other places he had yet to visit. A newspaper

25th November, 1974.

My dear Bhai Abdulkarimbhai and Bhai Alibhai,

Many thanks for Bhai Alibhai's letter dated 18th November, 1974 and for all the efforts which you both brothers have been making in finalizing the matter of Health Centres in Dar-es-salaam.

I have discussed your letter and the enclosures with Bhai Abdulkarimbhai in Karachi and I have decided to agree to donate the amount of Shs. 8,90,400 towards the four clinics in Dar-e-salaam. These will be as follows:-

1. <u>Ilala Health Centre</u>
   Delivery and Maternity Ward   Shs. 352,000.00

2. <u>Kipawa</u>
   Dispensary   Shs. 168,000.00

3. <u>Ukonga</u>
   Maternity and Antenatal Clinic   Shs. 185,200.00

4. <u>Tabata</u>
   Maternity and Antenatal Clinic   Shs. 185,200.00

It is my desire that the first mentioned Health Centre at Ilala should be in the name of your late sister whilst the other three smaller units should be in my own name. Further, in view of the escalating costs, if additional amounts are required to complete these four clinics and you are satisfied that these are genuine, then I leave to the discretion of you two brothers to increase the total amount by whatever is necessary.

I do hope that I have explained the position from my point of view properly to enable you to complete the clinics.

With our fond regards to all of you.

Yours affectionately,

Tayabali

Tayabali continued to spend his money on charities, despite the nationalisation of Karimjee properties a few years earlier.

Tayabali Karimjee around 1930.

cutting says that he had already travelled by air in East Africa. However, the fact that it was actually reported in the newspaper shows that this mode of transport was still very exceptional at that time.

In the 1940s, his position in the family business changed dramatically. Mohamedali died in 1940 and around that time Yusufali retired from the business for medical reasons (see page 52). The parent company's holding had become so large that it was divided into separate new companies. Tayabali was appointed the chairman of the Board of Directors of all companies and associated companies abroad. The total turnover of the companies was estimated at 'several million pounds a year'.[60] Because of these new responsibilities, he left the Legislative Council, where he had served more than 16 years (1932 - 1948).

In 1946 he left Zanzibar for Karachi. His mother, who was in Karachi, was ill and her eternal wish was to die with Tayabali by her side. Tayabali respected this. When his only child, Fizza, married in Zanzibar in 1960, he established the Tayabali Karimjee Educational Trust. This trust sponsored overseas scholarships for Tanzanians to go internationally renowned universities. Many of the alumni are the political and business leaders of Tanzania today. The Zanzibaris remembered Tayabali as follows: "It is true that Fizza is his only child, but he has not been content with one child. Therefore he adopted all of us in Zanzibar and Pemba." [61] In addition, he established the Fizza Adamjee Trust in London. The queen knighted him in 1955 for his charitable activities and contributions in public service. Last but not least, he played an important role in the establishment of Karimjee Hall (see page 133-135).

In 1958, Tayabali came to a crossroads in his life. His mother had died the year before and he wanted to devote more time to the family business in East Africa as well as his charities. It is said that he flipped a coin. If it was heads, he would stay in Karachi, and if it was tails he would move back to Zanzibar. So he moved to Zanzibar, based on chance alone. He built a beautiful house on the cliffs, which is now the State Guest House of Zanzibar.

The political events of the 1960s, however, would abruptly change his future. The Zanzibar Revolution (1964) resulted in the nationalisation of all Karimjee properties, such as copra factories, flourmills, land and houses. Tayabali's house was looted and all the contents, including jewellery, paintings and carpets were stolen. The current president's house at Kiponda formerly belonged to Sir Tayabali. The current House of Representatives used to be the Peoples Sports Club, one of Tayabali's charities (see further Appendix).

Tayabali went back to Karachi. He was seriously disappointed and could hardly cope with the realisation that the island that used to be his home, which he had helped to develop so much, was now in the grip of political anarchy. Despite these setbacks, he never abandoned his social responsibilities. Only a few years after the Tanganyika Government had nationalised much of the Karimjee properties in Dar es Salaam and Tanga (see page 132 and appendix), he agreed with his cousins Abdulkarim and Alibhai to sponsor the building of four health centres in Dar es Salaam.

While in Karachi, Tayabali unfortunately developed Alzheimer disease. The last years of his life were spent in Karachi. He would sit on a chair, just outside the gate of his home telling everyone: "I don't belong here; I am waiting for the bus to Zanzibar". He passed away in Karachi in 1987.

Sir Tayabali's tombstone in Karachi.

TAYABALI KARIMJEE

1897	Born in Zanzibar
1910	First visit to Europe
	His sister Sukan dies
1917	Marriage
1918	His father dies
1930 - 32	President of the Indian Association in Zanzibar
	Travels to Egypt with Abdulla Karimjee
1932	Appointed unofficial member of the Legislative Council
1934	Visits Ahmedabad
	becomes member of flying club
1937	Walks out of the Legislative Council, receives the order of the Brilliant Star of Zanzibar
	Chairman of all Karimjee Jivanjee companies
1948	Retires from the Legislative Council
	Knighted
	Opening of Karimjee Hall in Dar es Salaam (see page 134-135)
	Returns to Zanzibar
1964	Loses his Zanzibar home in the Zanzibar Revolution and returns to Karachi broken-hearted
1973	His wife dies
1987	Dies in Karachi

In this chapter we have seen that various Karimjees played an important role in politics and philanthropy. The experience of being a migrant as well as the Muslim background inspired the Karimjees to assume social responsibilities. The Karimjees served East Africa in many ways. They built hospitals, clinics and dispensaries. They contributed to schools, scholarships, the public library and the University of Dar es Salaam. And these are just the formal charities, for their philanthropy went far beyond that. Many times when they were compelled to give up buildings, land or other investments, they decided to donate them to charitible organisations, as in the case of the Maweni House (chapter 4). Sometimes they used their position in society to break the racial ties. Abdulla Karimjee built the Raskazone Swimming club. This club was open to all, Asians, Africans and Europeans alike, unlike the European yacht club in Tanga (chapter 4). Through their charities, the Karimjees provided a valuable supplement to the welfare assistance provided by the colonial administration and, after independence, by the Tanzanian State.

The Karimjees also made significant public service contributions. This was originally motivated by the injustices done to Asians by the colonial administration. Yusufali, Tayabali, Abdulla and Abdulkarim all took a stand against selfish actions taken by the British officials. Tayabali literally walked out of the Legislative Council after the Cloves Bill was passed. Nevertheless the Karimjees were recognised by the same people for their political abilities and contributions. Sir Tayabali Karimjee served on the Legislative Council of Zanzibar for 16 years and for two years as the president of the Indian Association. Abdulkarim Karimjee was probably the political lion amongst the Karimjees. He was the first elected non - white Mayor of Dar es Salaam. He was active in the East African Central Legislative Council and the Tanganyika Legislative Council and eventually became the first Speaker of Parliament in 1961 after Tanzania declared independence (see portrait chapter 5). The political activities would continue, most notably those of Amir Karimjee, who became Assistant Minister of Trade & Industry in the first pre - independence government.[62] In all these activities, these individuals had to find a balance between their business, the family and public.

CHAPTER 7

Explaining the Past While Looking at the Future

What is the secret of the Karimjee Jivanjee family? What makes them outstanding, entrepreneurial survivors? How and why did they continue, where others gave up? What were the decisive changes in history that shaped their fortunes? In short, what was the driving force behind this remarkable business history? These afterthoughts highlight a few fascinating historical moments that twisted the Karimjee Jivanjee history, as we know it. This chapter discusses some of the latest developments in the Karimjee Jivanjee business and family history. The recent management decisions have been taken based on a vision of the future for the family and its business. Therefore, this book concludes with a glimpse of the past and a glance at the future.

One of the first pioneering achievements of the Karimjee Jivanjee family was – without a doubt – crossing the *kalapani* (black waters) of the Indian Ocean in a dhow. Jivanjee Buddhaboy was definitely not the first family elder in Mandvi to send one of his sons to Zanzibar, but anyone with a small child can imagine what it must feel like to send your son abroad. Almost two centuries ago it was an extremely dangerous and daring journey in a dhow to an unknown world with a different language and culture with very little means of communication. The more informally organised South Asian migration from West India to East Africa would not commence until around the 1880s. Thus, Buddhaboy travelled well before the major South Asian chain migration to East Africa started and became somewhat more organised. Father and son (Jivanjee) were therefore extremely courageous and entrepreneurial.

In the early 19th century, there were perhaps 300 Bohras living in Zanzibar. Even in those days, this was a tiny community. Jivanjee was able to set up his own business and within a few years, in 1825, he established Karimjee Jivanjee & Co. This was a remarkable achievement, but the fact that he divided the business

Old ways of transport, in the 30s.

among his brothers Pirbhai and Esmailjee in 1861 was even more significant. This was very uncommon in those days, but for some reason he must have felt more comfortable discovering his own course of life and business. The Hurumzi house where the family lived together still stands in Zanzibar. But through the ages the connection with other parts of the family has vanished. In fact, in a business directory from 1909, the author was not aware that Karimjee Jivanjee & Co. was related to Esmailjee Jivanjee & Co.[63]

The fact was that Karimjee Jivanjee & Co. was established and all members of the family would play their part in the business. The family acquired a growing number of trading licenses and their trade grew beyond the East African interior. Between 1880 and 1922 most Indian traders expanded and became successful and those who did not manage to do so started to work for other businesses. However, very few Asian business families would end up doing business with East Asia (including Japan) as well as Europe (especially the UK and Germany) and the East African Coast as well the African interior. The family also diversified into land in the early 1920s. The coffee, tea and sisal estates ran profitably in the initial decades, but this was nothing compared to the sisal boom of the early 1950s. Within a few years, millionaires were made and Tanga became the hometown of the most prosperous period in the history of Tanganyika.

Thereafter, the Karimjee Jivanjee family carried out their second major pioneering act when they diversified from trades to estates. From a business historian's perspective, we may ask ourselves whether this diversification was due to an instinctive foresight, innovative action, just luck, hard work or something else. These 'great questions' often have multiple, sometimes mutually contradictory, answers. In addition, the results cannot be attributed to one person. However, we can highlight two persons in particular here. One is Sir Yusufali Karimjee, the 'grand' explorer in the family who travelled from East Africa to India, East Asia to Japan and back, looking for new trading opportunities as well reconfirming existing ones. In addition, he was the one who bought 'Enemy Properties', i.e. land and buildings that had belonged to Germans before the war. Of course his business instinct helped him to build up the Karimjee Trading Empire and he must have foreseen the importance of land. He may have listened to Fatemben, who also foresaw a big future for the Karimjees in agriculture. Or was it the Greek landowner who advised him to buy land during Yusufali's afternoon walk? It is difficult to say, but often, hard work, foresight and being there at the right time and place come together.

The second person to highlight here is Abdulla Mohamedali Karimjee, who became the Managing Director of the estates and the Director of Karimjee Jivanjee Estates Ltd. Buying land with the prospect of generating profits is one thing, but turning the land into a smooth and well-organised agricultural business system is another. Abdulla has to be credited with doing precisely that. Without any previous experience in agriculture, he was literally 'sent' to Tanga' to run the estates. He hired managers from Ceylon, India and elsewhere to assist him. He had to learn from experience, through 'trial and error' because the estate business was in its infancy at the time. However, he had inherited enough of the Karimjee pioneering spirit and genes to fulfil this task with courage. He eventually became the most important non-white estate manager and owner in Tanga. After he had established various trading organisations, he became an important sisal baron in the whole of East Africa, and he played his role on the sidelines in the efforts to overcome the colour bar for both himself and others.

His success in business was also based on the aforementioned combination of hard work, innovation and entrepreneurship, and being there at the right time and the right place. It is beyond any doubt that the pioneering work on the estates was pure hard work, including physical work convincing the managers and others of the prospects as well. The Karimjees did not invest a large sum of their capital in estates. This was just very rational business acumen in not risking too much in new ventures, but first seeing for yourself whether you can find your niche in the new business environment. Abdulla certainly managed to do that. Last but not least, no one could have foreseen the impact of the Korean War on the price of sisal in the world market. As we have seen, millionaires were made almost overnight. This had a considerable impact on the business success of the Karimjee Jivanjee family.

The third pioneering act was of a different order. Building a business is one thing, but surviving where others fail is something else entirely. The Karimjees survived the most difficult era in Tanganyika's business history. Political factors, war and ideological issues shaped most of this history. The Zanzibar Revolution of 1964 led to the nationalisation of the Karimjee properties and businesses on the island. In addition, the psychosocial impact was immeasurable. If you have spent so much of your life running your businesses, supporting the local communities through charities and being active in politics, the 'act of nationalisation' cuts the umbilical cord between you and your place of birth, your roots and your identity. This is precisely what happened to Sir Tayabali Karimjee, who happened to be a fourth generation Zanzibar-born Karimjee, and despite his intentions and wishes otherwise, he was forced to retire in Karachi while dreaming of Zanzibar.

Nevertheless, more dark clouds were blown in the direction of Tanganyika on the eve of independence and in its aftermath. Before the independent era, the worldwide influences of the different political economic ideologies played an important role in the building of a new nation state. One of the questions posed was whether Tanganyika should follow a more socialist pattern, or a capitalist pattern. It is now known, for example, that Kenya chose an African Capitalist way, whereas Tanganyika chose an African Socialist Democracy, named Ujamaa. No one foresaw, however, the anti-Asian nature of Uganda under General Idi Amin. In 1967 and 1971, most of the Karimjee properties and businesses were nationalised. In the same year most Karimjees, especially those with children, left the country and at one point only three remained in East Africa. These three were able to keep the business alive, and in fact that is all that was possible. The champion of managers who had to navigate through this difficult political and economic arena was without doubt Abdulkarim. He died in 1977, but the family was able – once again – to stand up and find others to fill the gaps that he left behind (Alibhai, Anver, and Hatim). In true, family business tradition, there was enough management calibre – whatever happened in society – to keep the business going.

The last in the line of major political changes was the liberalisation programme of President Benjamin Mkapa from the 1990s onwards. These were turbulent years once again but with a positive twist. On the one hand, the Karimjees lost their flagship, Karimjee Agriculture Ltd. Despite tremendous efforts it was not economical to keep the estates going. On the other hand, new ventures were started. In the 1990s the Karimjees had diversified into several new investments in advertising and commodity exports. Karimjee Marketing Ltd was established in 1998 to buy cashew nuts in the coastal and southern regions for export to India via Karimjee Jivanjee & Co. (UK) Ltd. The company exported other commodities such as sawn timber, pigeon peas and pulses and annatto seed and imported wheat flour. In addition, a joint venture was established in 1990 with one of Kenya's leading advertising agencies to form ScanAd Tanzania. This company was started in anticipation of a more competitive market economy, including the liberalisation of the media, as well as to cater for the marketing needs of Toyota Tanzania. Within five years it became Tanzania's number one advertising agency.

Nevertheless, when Karimjee Agriculture went under, one lesson that the family had learnt was to "stick to the knitting" (a management term that means that companies should concentrate their energies on what they do best). As a result, ScanAd was sold back to its Kenyan parent company and Karimjee Marketing was closed down. It had become clear that Dar es Salaam remained the centre of the mother company, Karimjee Jivanjee Ltd., and the directors agreed to concentrate

CHAPTER 7 · EXPLAINING THE PAST WHILE LOOKING AT THE FUTURE

Picture taken at the annual family meeting in London in 1998.

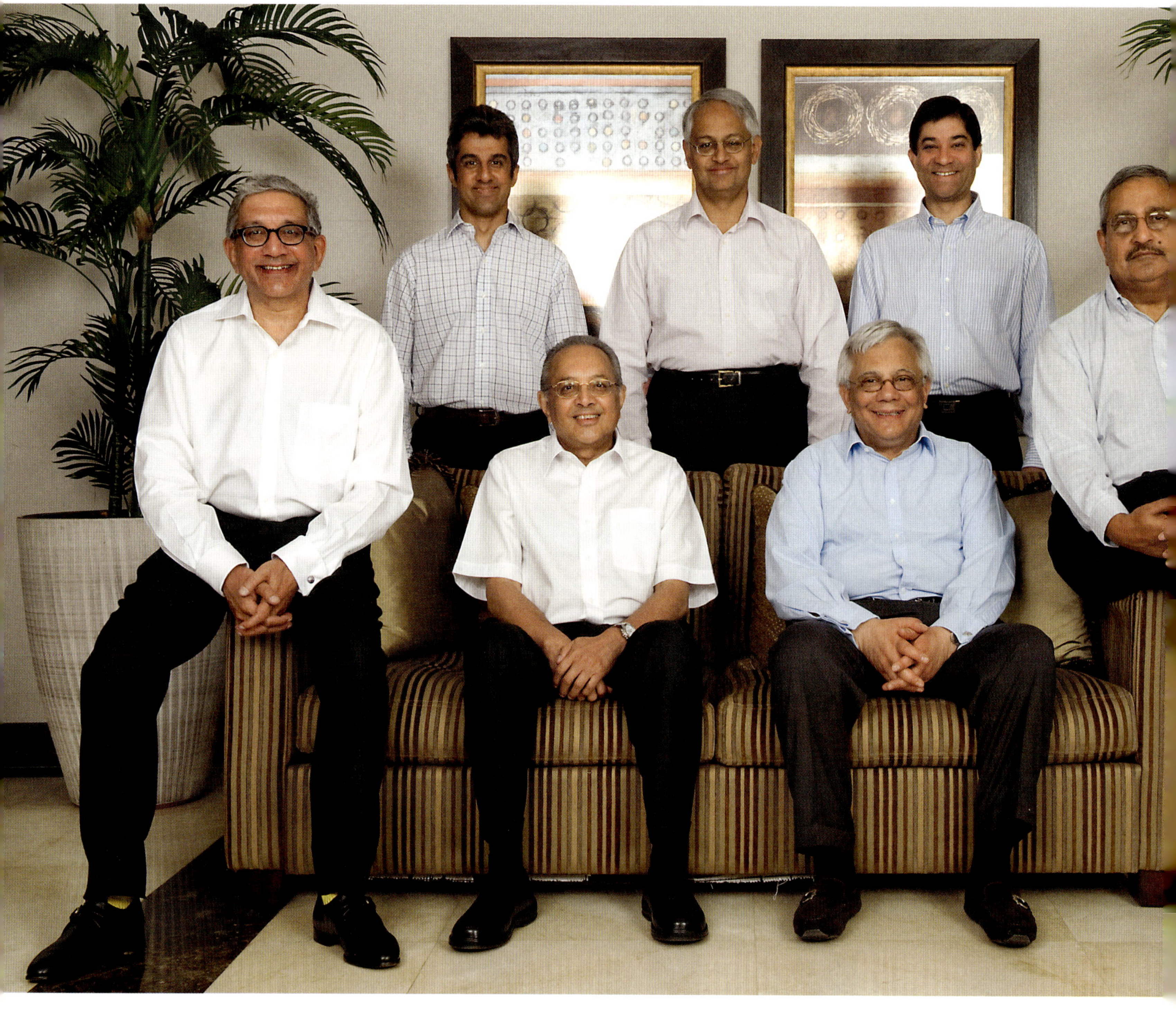

CHAPTER 7 · EXPLAINING THE PAST WHILE LOOKING AT THE FUTURE

their investments in Tanzania. Future investments would focus on franchise marketing in Tanzania in a market and environment that the family knew and where they had a good reputation. This made Karimjee Jivanjee a local business owned by a global family.

The major franchise was – and still is – Toyota. The Karimjees had promised Toyota Japan that they would make major improvements in general management, in marketing and new vehicle sales, in the performance of the spare parts division, in expanding and improving dealer networks and in service & repair performance. Mahmood Karimjee was appointed to the Board of Directors in 1993 and he became the Managing Director of Toyota Tanzania Ltd. in 1997. The company had once again changed its name from International Motors Ltd. to Toyota Tanzania Ltd. at the request of Toyota Japan as part of its global strategy.

In line with the family tradition, the new manager had no prior experience in the car sales business. He was Sir Yusufali's grandson, Amir's son, and Hatim's younger brother by 10 years. He had been educated in England and Switzerland at L'Ecole Hôtelière de Lausanne, had spent many years in the hotel industry and had more recently built Migration Camp, one of the most beautiful luxury tented lodges in the Serengeti National Park. However, with his grandfather's instinct, he was able to work within the rapidly changing East African economy to not only fulfil the promises made to Toyota, but also to develop the business to a much higher level.

Under the new management and with new investments, Toyota Tanzania rapidly took off and became Tanzania's leading car distributor. Sales increased from 350 new vehicles per year in 1987 to nearly 2000 vehicles in 2005. In 1987/88 the 500 shilling banknote was Tanzania's largest banknote and it became known as the "Pajero" because the Mitsubishi Pajero was at that time Tanzania's most popular luxury car. By 1989, however, the Pajero banknote was forgotten and Toyota became the market leader.

Current Directors, (left to right) backrow;
Arif Karimjee, Azim Karimjee, Riaz Adamjee.
Frontrow; Mahmood A. Karimjee,
Hatim A. Karimjee - Chairman,
Latif A. Karimjee - Vice Chairman,
Nazim Karimjee.

The company had a market share of nearly 50% of all new vehicles sold in Tanzania and continued to make good profits. The company was rated by the Tanzania Revenue Authority as one of its major tax payers. Toyota Tanzania had also acquired the Yamaha Motorcycles agency in 1992. This agency was managed through its subsidiary City Motors Limited. Other Toyota family agencies were added in 2001, such as Daihatsu Cars and Hino Trucks.

The turbulent years were over for the time being and the family leaders realised that it was time to continue building on and improving family unity. This was not an easy task as many family members now lived in different parts of the world, including Britain, Mauritius, Pakistan, Dubai, the USA, Germany and France. In September 2004 the board of directors discussed various ways of keeping the family together and being more responsive to their needs. Among other things, it was agreed to organise an annual family reunion in London.. The first reunion was held in 1996 and the reunion has been held every year since then. The reunion lunch brings together between 60 and 100 family members ranging from senior members to newborn babies. Gifts are presented at the reunion in recognition of major anniversaries and birthdays, as well as marriages and births. These reunions are designed to keep the family together and to prevent fragmentation over time.

It was also agreed that a family council would be established. This council would advise family members on shareholder issues and planning for succession. It was clear that different groups within the family had different interests and different associations with the family's businesses. Many were just very small shareholders with sometimes no more than five per cent of the shares. Some of them might be keen to sell their shares to invest in other personal priorities. This situation was also complicated by the fact that most family members were not available for face-to-face meetings in Africa and conclusions were often based on second-hand information. The family council was established to facilitate the various interests in a transparent way and to assist with the sale of shares, share valuation, and transfer mechanisms.

Family members were encouraged to visit Tanzania and see the country for themselves because the younger generation had lost touch with their roots. Some might have been familiar with 'stories from Africa' but had either never visited Tanzania, or had visited more than 30 years ago. Some of the older members of the family had not returned after they left in the late 1960s or early 1970s. As a result, a visiting scheme was drawn up in which family members were encouraged and given incentives to visit together with their children and grandchildren. However, reconnecting with regional origins ought to include the historical roots as well, so it was agreed that a history book would be commissioned to preserve the family's amazing history over the last 200 years. This book was designed to reconnect the family with its shared past in Africa.

Ultimately, an even more challenging aim was to encourage younger family members to consider a career in the family business in Tanzania. Two packages were established for this purpose: a three-month study visit and a two-year graduate training package. The short study visit was designed to provide an all-round overview of Tanzania and the working environment. The longer working package was a career opening for graduates and would focus on a particular profession. This principle of 'learning on the job' reflects a long tradition in South Asian family businesses. Some of today's managing directors worked as youngsters for the company that they are now managing. Acquiring knowledge from within the company is often an additional asset for future managers. It is frequently one of the key success factors in family businesses. The idea was that the younger family members would learn to recognise local working conditions and become familiar with local living conditions. Some younger members of the family have taken up this challenge.

The Karimjee charities needed to be revived for future plans. The family's good reputation was partly due to its honesty in business and partly due to its charitable contributions and overseas scholarships. All of these charitable contributions were funded by corporate profits or by endowment funds created more than 40 years ago. Corporate profits dried up in the 1970s thanks to nationalisation or adverse business conditions. In the 1950s the Sir Tayabali Karimjee Education Trust was able to educate at least ten graduate students per year but by the year 2000 the Trust was not able to educate even one student because tuition fees and the cost of living had risen astronomically and the endowment fund income had fallen. There was clearly a need to reactivate and refinance the charities. In 2005 the directors proposed merging the family's myriad of trusts and establishing a new super trust called 'The Karimjee Jivanjee Foundation'. There were six charitable trusts to be merged. They all had their own objectives, assets and means of income:

- Sir Tayabali Karimjee Educational Trust
- Tayabali H.A. Karimjee Trust
- Yusufali Charitable Trust – Tanzania
- Sir Yusufali Charitable Trust – Kenya
- Mohamedali A.K. Jivanjee Charity Trust
- Mohamedali Trust – London

The main objectives of the original trusts were either educatio or general charity. This was in line with the traditions of the founder members of the family as well as the charitable principles of Islam. Education meant providing scholarships to gifted students, and general charity involved building schools, hospitals, dispensaries, mosques, community centres, as well as providing medical treatment or equipment, etc.

The primary objective of the new Karimjee Jivanjee Foundation is to provide scholarships to gifted Tanzanian students to study in Tanzania where their parents are unable to meet the costs of their children's education. Other charitable needs may also be considered on their merits. The philosophy behind the Karimjee charities is based upon a saying from the Rubbaiyat of Omar Khyaam: "It is not giving if you profit by the giving". People who seek to bolster their ego or to gain some political popularity far too often make so-called charitable donations.

We are now looking forward to the sixth and seventh generations of Karimjees building upon the achievements of their great-, great-, great-, and great grandfathers….

Today, the Karimjee companies are healthy, flourishing companies, with the Toyota business as the figurehead. This is an achievement without parallel in East African business history. The prospects are good and the history of the Karimjee family has shown that they can meet the challenge of almost every political and economic adversity possible. If we look at the family tree we see that they have produced numerous offspring who have been educated in the four corners of the world. It is tempting to assume that among them new merchant princes have been born. And with this book in their hand those princes will have one foot in their history from which they step with their other foot forward into the future.

Acknowledgements and sources

Private businesses are not renowned for their willingness to lay bare their insights to researchers. However, for the purpose of my research, I was given free access to all the available sources, records and correspondences related to the business history of the Karimjee Jivanjee family. In the spring of 2006, the Board of Directors of the holding company, Karimjee Jivanjee & Co., decided that a business history of the company and its family should be written. The research started in 2007. The directors of the company made available their business correspondence and the annual reports of various companies, and shared their invaluable business insight and experience with me.

The official records of a business organisation seldom tell the complete story. Interviews with various members of the family (males and females through the various generations) were conducted to fill in any gaps in knowledge. Some were interviewed more than three times. In this context, I would especially like to mention Hatim Karimjee, Latif Karimjee, and Mahmood Karimjee, who all sat through series of long probing interviews. These are the current champions of the Karimjee Jivanjee family business. It is very likely that some of their offspring will continue to maintain the excellent name of the family. In addition, Carrim A. Currimjee shared his insights from the 'Mauritius' perspective. Furthermore, the family acted as contacts between managers, accountants and employees of the firm.

It is impossible for me to repay the intellectual debt I owe to my professional colleagues and friends. These include Ned Alpers, Garreth Austen, Dick Douwes, Claude Markovits, Henk Schulte Nordholt and Alex van Stipriaan and many others whose names I cannot possibly mention without making this list unduly long. I am also indebted to the Faculty of History and Arts of the Erasmus University, which allowed me to work on this project in my research time. In addition, I am thankful for the librarians and staff of the British Library, especially of the African and Asian sections, the National Archives (UK), the Tanganyika National Archives, and the Zanzibar Archives.

I am most grateful to all these individuals and organisations. Without their help, this work would never have been completed.

Gijsbert Oonk
Rotterdam, July 2009

PRIMARY SOURCES

Public Record Office

- CO 323/820/13 1920 Return of claims
  CO 323/1911/2 1950 Mr and Mrs Karimjee
  CO 323/1930/11 1951 Mr and Mrs Karimjee
- Kirk's survey of Zanzibar & Dominions in 1870, Foreign Office 44/1936. Foreign Office 881/6710. Excerpt from the speech by Hon. Tayabali H.A. Karimjee at the Legislative Council meeting of 18 December 1936

British Library

- Yusufali Esmailjee Jivanjee, *Memorandum on the Report of the Commission on Agriculture*, 1923. Poona 1924.
- K.P.S. Menon, *Report on the Marketing Legislation in Tanganyika, Uganda and Kenya*, Government of India Press 1934.
- Somerset Playne, *East Africa (British). Its History, People, Commerce, Industries, and Resources,* published by the Foreign and Colonial Compiling and Publishing Company, 1909, pp. 420-423.
- Notes on the Tea Estates in Africa, compiled by Wilson, Smithett & Co.,Published by Thomas Skinner & Co, London 1954.
- Tanganyika Merchants Princes', *Caltext Star*, volume (3) 9, 1952, pp. 4-7.

Newspapers

- *Samarch Jubilee issue 1929; 1936.*
- *The Tanga Post and East Coast Advertiser*
- *The Tanganyika Herald*
- *The Zanzibar Voice*
- *The Tanganyika Opinion*

Family records

- My Life: Handwritten record (Gujarati) from Fazelabbas Esmailjee. Probably written in 1905.
- Annual meetings of the Board of Directors of various companies, including:
  Karimjee Jivanjee Estates Ltd., Tanga.
  Karimjee Jivanjee & Co. Ltd., Dar es Salaam
  Karimjee Jivanjee Properties, Ltd., Dar es Salaam
  International Motor Mart, Ltd., Dar es Salaam
  Karimjee Trading Co. Ltd., Bombay
  Karimjee Properties Ltd., Bombay
  Tanganyika Sisal Marketing Association, Ltd., Tanga
  TASMA Finance Corporation Ltd., Tanga.
- Citation by Dr C.K. Omari, to present to Abdulkarim Yusufali Alibhai Karimjee for the award of the degree of Doctor of Law from the University of Dar es Salaam, 1973.

Zanzibar Archives

- ZNA AB 2/150 Hassanali Karimjee Jivanjee Hospital

Interviews

- Karimjee family:
  Arif Karimjee, Fizza Hakim Adamjee, Hatim Karimjee, Latif Karimjee, Nazim Karimjee, Mahmood Karimjee, Ruby Karimjee, Zaibun Karimjee, Rati Khandawala, Shabnam Karimjee, Hilal Karimjee, Yasmin Karimjee.
- Currimjee family:
  Carrim A Currimjee, Abbas Currimjee, Ashraf Currminjee.

Others

- Mustafa Alibhai (in-law)
- Taher Ali (legal advisors) and Zehra Taher Ali (his wife)
- Fakhru Bharmal (in-law) Ruby Bharmal (his wife)
- Haruna Ali (former servant to Alibhai Karimjee Jivanjee)

LIST OF SOURCES RELATED TO THE HISTORY OF THE KARIMJEE JIVANJEE FAMILY

- Manilal Dewani (former Mayor of Dar es Salaam)
- Hiren Desai (chartered accountant)
- Al Noor Kassam (representative of the HH Aga Khan in Dar es Salaam, former Cabinet Minister)
- Vinoo Somaiya (former chartered accountant to the Karimjee Jivanjee family)
- Kitwana S. Kondo (former Mayor of Dar es Salaam)

SECONDARY LITERATURE

- Bates, Darell, *A Gust of Plumes. A Biography of Lord Twining of Godalming and Tanganyika*, London, Sydney 1972.
- Burton, Richard F, *Zanzibar City, Island and Coast*, (1872) reprint 2003, University Press of the Pacific 2003.
- Christie, James, *Cholera Epidemics in East Africa. An account of the several diffusions of the disease in that country from 1821 till 1872, with an outline of the geography, ethnology, and trade connections of the regions through which the epidemics passed*, Macmillan London 1876.
- Guillebaud, C.W., *An Economic Survey of the Sisal Industry of Tanganyika*, London 1966.
- Gregory Robert G., *The Rise and Fall of Philanthropy in East Africa. The Asian Contribution,* Transaction Publishers, London, 1992.
- Gregory, Robert G., *Quest for Equality. Asian Politics in East Africa*, 1900-1967, Oriental Longman 1993.
- Gregory Robert, G, *India and East Africa: A History of Race Relations within the British Empire*, 1890-1939, Oxford 1971.
- Gregory Robert, G., *South Asians in East Africa. An Economic and Social History, 1890-1980*, Boulder: Westview Press, 1993.
- Gregory Robert, G., Co-operation and collaboration in colonial East Africa: The Asians' Political Role, 1890- 1965*, African Affairs* 80 (319), 1981, pp. 259-273.
- Hitchcock, Sir Eldred, *The Sisal Industry of Tanganyika*, Reprinted from the Tanganyika Trade Bulletin, 1955.
- Lock, G.W., *Sisal: 25 years of Sisal Research*, London 1962.
- Maliyamkono, T.L. and Bagachwa, M.S.D. *The Second Economy in Tanzania*, James Currey, 1990.
- Oonk, Gijsbert, South Asians in East Africa (1880-1920) With a Particular Focus on Zanzibar. Towards a historical explanation of economic success of a middlemen minority. *Journal of African and Asian Studies*, 2006, pp. 57-89.
- Oonk, Gijsbert, South Asians in East Africa. Contribution in *The Encyclopaedia of the Indian Diaspora*. Edited by P. Reeves, Brij Lal and Rajesh Rai, eds, Singapore: Éditions Didier Millet 2006.
- Oonk, Gijsbert, 'After Shaking his hand, start counting your fingers. Trust and Images in Indian business networks, East Africa 1900-2000', republished in Geoffrey Jones and Dan Wadhwani, in *Entrepreneurship and Global Capitalism*, Edward Elgar Press 2006.
- Oonk, Gijsbert., Gujarati Business Communities in East Africa. Success and Failure Stories, *Economic and Political Weekly*, 2005 Vol XL (20), pp. 2077-2082.
- Oonk, Gijsbert, 'After Shaking his hand, start counting your fingers. Trust and Images in Indian business networks, East Africa 1900-2000', *Itinerario* 18 (3) 2004, pp. 70-88.
- Oonk, Gijsbert, The Changing Culture of the Hindu Lohana Community in East Africa,*Contemporary Asian Studies*, 13 (1) 2004, pp. 7-23.
- Oonk, Gijsbert, *Asians in East Africa. Images Pictures and Portraits.* Sca producties 2004.
- Oonk, Gijsbert, (ed) *Global Indian Diasporas. Trajectories of theory and Migration.* Amsterdam University Press 2007.
- Patel, Zarina, *Challenge to Colonialism. The Struggle of Alibhai Mulla Jeevanjee for Equal Rights in Kenya*, Mombasa 1997.
- Pandit, Shanti (ed.), *Asians in East and Central Africa*, Nairobi,

- Panco 1963.
- Parpart, L., and Rostgaard, M., *The Practical Imperialist. Letters from a Danish Planter in East Africa, 1888-1906,* Brill Leiden, Boston, 2007.
- Tom Peters and Robert Waterman, *In Search for Excellence*, New York 1982.
- Ramchandani R.R., *Uganda Asians. The end of an Enterprise,* Bombay United Asians Publications, Bombay 1976.
- Rau, Uwe and Mwalim A. Mwalim, *Doors of Zanzibar*, HSP publications London/Zanzibar 1998.
- Salvadori, Cynthia. *Through Open Doors. A view of Asian Cultures in Kenya*, Nairobi 1989 (1983) 2nd edition, pp. 254-269.
- Salvadori, Cynthia, *They Came in Dhows,* three volumes. Published from Nairobi 1996.
- Voigt-Graff, C., *Asian Communities in Tanzania. A Journey Through Past and Present Times,* Hamburg 1998.
- Westcott, Nicholas, 'The East African Sisal Industry, 1929-1949: The Marketing of a Colonial Commodity during Depression and War, *The Journal of African History*, 25 (4) 1984, pp. 445-461.

LIST OF LOST PROPERTIES IN ZANZIBAR AND TANGANYIKA

Nationalised Karimjee Properties in Zanzibar

- *The Peoples Bank of Zanzibar.*
Address: House 180/181 Behind to the Portuguese Fort Mohamedali Karimjee bought it between 1904 and 1907. It was nationalised in 1964.
- *The Hurumzi House.*
Address: Hurumzi 239. Yusufali bought this house probably from Tharia Topan.

This building is in the midst of Stone Town and just recently became part of 236 Hurumzi Hotel (Formerly Emmerson and Green Hotel. Nationalised in 1964.
- *Tayabali's first house*
This house is currently in deteriorated condition, next to Sultan's Palace Museum. Nationalised in 1964.
- *Tayabali's house at Kiponda.*
Built in the Spanish style and it is now one of the residences of the President of Zanzibar. Its design is based on Abdalla Karimjee's house in Tanga. Nationalised in 1964.
- *Hassanali Hospital*, now it is extended considerably Near Mnazi Moja Ground. Nationalised in 1964.
- Peoples Sports Club which was called the *Karimjee Sports Club*. Charity of Sir Tayabali Karimjee, it is currently used as The Zanzibar House of Representatives
Address: - Opp. Mnazi Moja Ground. Nationalised in 1964.
- *Fumba House* (picture below).
Currently the President's guest house. Nationalised in 1964.

LIST OF SOURCES RELATED TO THE HISTORY OF THE KARIMJEE JIVANJEE FAMILY

LIST OF NATIONALISED PROPERTIES

The following three spreads contain a list of the nationalised properties formerly belonging to the Karimjee family or one of their companies. Most properties were nationalised after the 22nd of April 1971, as a result of the 'Act to empower the President to acquire certain Buildings' (see chapter five). But a few had been taken by the mid nineteen sixties. Most buildings were acquired in Dar es Salaam, in the table referred to as DSM. Others were acquired in Tanga. Whenever possible the original plot numbers and the change of plot numbers are mentioned. The original addresses are mentioned as well as the size of the plot and or the buildings. But most of it has been changed over the years. >>

TOWN	FILE NO	PLOT NO	C.E.P. LOT NO	NEW PLOT NO	BLOCK NO	STREET
A DSM	1		4	19	186024	CITY DRIVE - IML BUILDING
A DSM	2		33	28	186021	RAILWAY STREET/MAIN AVENUE
A DSM	3	331/33	43	15	186024	MKWEPU STREET (EXPLORERS HOUSE)
A DSM	4		121	2	186027	SAMORA AVENUE
A DSM	5	107/11 (101)	119	1 (4)	186027	SAMORA AVENUE/MIRAMBO STREET
A DSM	6	322/32	12	4	186024	SAMORA AVENUE/MKWEPU STREET
A DSM	7	638/57		86	186016	SAMORA AVENUE/SELOUS STREET (CENTRAL HTL)
A DSM	8	230/59		84	186016	SAMORA AVENUE (J.HAMIR)
A DSM	9	106	22	6	186022	SAMORA AVENUE/MOROGORO ROAD
A DSM	10	265/122	45	3	186022	SAMORA AVENUE
A DSM	11	123/50	46	2	186022	SAMORA AVENUE
A DSM	12	124	44	1	186022	SAMORA AVENUE/ALGERIA STREET
A DSM	13	170/129	41	17	186021	RAILWAY STREET/ARAB STREET(NKURUMAH ST)
A DSM	14	454/160		40	186013	GEREZANI/NKURUMAH STREET
A DSM	15	139		10	186015	INDIA STREET/AGGREY STREET (H.VISRAM BUILDING)
A DSM	16	68/98		14	186016	MOSQUE STREET
A DSM	17	188/25	26	30	186017	BRIDGE STREET/HARDING STREET
A DSM	18	2187/12	29/30	3	186007	INGLES/JAMHURI STREET
A DSM	19	105/27	108	7	186054	AZIKIWE STREET
A DSM	20	146/47	111	2	186055	UPANGA ROAD
A DSM	21	40/48	110	3	186057	UPANGA ROAD (OHIO STREET)
A DSM	22	140 & 147/47	113	3 & 4	186055	OHIO STREET (CRICKET PITCH)
A DSM	23	2356/47	112	9 & 20	186055	OHIO STREET (ORIENT CLUB)
A DSM	24			17	186053	KISUTU STREET/MRIMA STREET/TITI STREET
A DSM	25	146	55	17	186166	UPANGA - OCEAN ROAD
A DSM	25	137	55	8	186166	UPANGA - UPANGA ROAD
A DSM	25	117	55	33	186166	UPANGA - UPANGA ROAD
A DSM	25	381	55	56	186168	UPANGA - JAMAT FLATS 41-56
A DSM	25	118	55	32	186166	UPANGA - UPANGA ROAD
A DSM	25	383	55	45	186168	UPANGA - JAMAT FLATS 41-56
A DSM	25	379	55	58	186168	UPANGA - INC 59 NOW
A DSM	25	378	55	46	186168	UPANGA - JAMAT FLATS 41-56
A DSM	25	369	55	21	186168	UPANGA - OCEAN ROAD
A DSM	25	145	55	16	186166	UPANGA - OCEAN ROAD
A DSM	25	164	55	48	186180	UPANGA - JAMAT FLATS 41-56
A DSM	26	1508/5	762	32 & 33	186045	SEAVIEW
A DSM	27	69		23	186035	HAILE SELASSIE ROAD
A DSM	29		963			SHAMBA 75 FLUR IV/PUGU ROAD
A/C DSM	1	62/129				NKRUMAH STREET
A/C DSM	3	145/47				UPANGA ROAD
A/C DSM	4	108/11		4	186027	MIRAMBO STREET
A/C DSM	5	1524/101		53	186016	INDIA/MOROGORO
B DSM	1	272/30		49	186017	SAMORA AVENUE (SPLENDID HOTEL) EXTELCOMM
B DSM	2	373/25		27	186017	INDIRA GANDHI STREET/BRIDGE STREET
B DSM	3	519/14		14	186006	UPANGA/KISUTU STREET
B DSM	4			48	186017	SAMORA AVENUE (SPLENDID HOTEL) EXTELCOMM
B DSM	5	68		14	186035	HAILE SELASSIE ROAD

TOTAL

NATIONALISED PROPERTIES

TITLE DEED NO	SQ. FT.	DATA AQUIRED	COMMENTS
	35.948	23/04/71	KARIMJEE JIVANJEE
7120	12.957	17/06/69	OPEN SPACE
7026	6.123	23/04/71	EXPORTERS TRADING/AL SHAAF BARGAIN CENTRE
7700	22.098	29/06/71	IFM BUILDING & RECENT OFFICE BLOCK
7704	11.614	25/06/71	EXISTING. (107/11)-NEW CONSTRUCTION ON THE WAY
6834	6.242	23/04/71	METROLEX/VAYLE FLORIST & 5/6 OTHERS/SHIVACOM
6509	6.929	29/03/65	GULHAMHUSEIN BROTHERS - DEMOLISHED
9725	3.167	23/04/71	RENDEZVOUS REST.&TZ MEAT(NOWMONEYLINK BUREAU DE CHANGE)
6729	18.132	23/04/71	RECENTLY DEMOLISHED SITE FOR NEW NIC/PFP BUILDING
7755	13.132	23/04/71	GM SULEMANJI & SONS (265/122) / DEMOLISHED
	10.872	23/04/71	GESTETNER/MIN. EDUCATION/CIC/DEMOLISHED
7756	9.720	23/04/71	LUKU SHOP-CURRENTLY UNDER RENOVATION
7119	11.242	SOLD	AFINA/CHICKEN INN (170/129)
6510	10.206	13/08/71	3 BUNGALOWS, 2 WITH SHOPS
2770	5.499	23/04/71	JARIWALLA STORES/PRISON SHOPS/ANKO TZ LTD
7024	2.268	14/12/71	BUSINESS TIMES/MANEK TRADING/HASSANALI ISSA/NEEMA ENTP
7121	12.469	29/03/65	OPEN SPACE CAR PARK
8091	88.036	14/12/71	MERRYWATER/VIOO GLASS(2386-31/12)/OPEN SPACE
7753	7.500	25/06/71	EXISTING 105/27
7705	18.567	29/01/69	BARCLAYS BANK
7752	63.109	25/06/71	AKIBA COMMERCIAL BANK
7758	29.278	14/02/69	NEW CONSTRUCTION ON THE WAY/MOVENPICK CAR PARK
7754	22.950	25/06/71	IMMIGRATION
10243	23.173	16/06/69	SCHOOL & C.M.C. HOLDING - UWT/MAKTABA ST.
	18.115	8/1/1965	RESIDENCE HOUSE/NHC FLAT
	15.970	8/1/1965	AMI HOUSE-OPP. ALCOVE RESTAURANT - SAMORA AVENUE
	13.717	8/1/1965	PRIVATE OWNERS
	10.888	8/1/1965	12 FLATS NHC& PRIVATE OWNERS
	15.419	8/1/1965	EMBASSY OF THE REPUBLIC OF RWANDA
	10.888	8/1/1965	SEMI DETACHED HOUSE
	13.313	8/1/1965	BLOCK OF FLATS/NHC
	10.888	8/1/1965	SEMI DETACHED HOUSE/NHC
	14.779	8/1/1965	RESIDENCE HOUSE/NHC FLAT
	17.457	8/1/1965	RESIDENCE HOUSE/NHC FLAT
	10.888	5/4/1965	SEMI DETACHED HOUSE
7116	64.623	29/05/71	COWIE CONSULT/NEW BUILDING SUBDIVIDED PLOT INC 31 NOW
9770	51.028	21/05/71	OLD ARRIGONI/HAK FLAT
5980	6.969.600		NEW INDUSTRIAL AREA
	4.855	18/08/71	3 STOREY BUILDING WITH FLATS & NATIONAL TYRE - OPP CHOX
7750	43.950	21/05/71	TRANSAFRICA CONSORTIUM
6819	14.499	21/05/71	101/4 EXISTING. HALF PLOT TAKEN FOR ENTRANCE TO A4
2730	2.772	23/04/71	DEMOLISHED-NEW CONSTRUCTION ON THE WAY
	13.582	23/04/71	EXTELCOMM BUILDING
7083	12.648	27/04/71	DSM GLASS/PANDYA HOTEL - DEMOLISHED
7124	23.939	27/04/71	OPEN ENCLOSED YARD - NU -TEK ENGINEERS
	13.582	23/04/71	EXTELCOMM BUILDING
	54.066	21/05/71	A.K.M.A.KARIMJEE

7.872.697

TOWN	FILE NO	PLOT NO	C.E.P. LOT NO	NEW PLOT NO	BLOCK NO	STREET
DSM	1	331/33				MKWEPU STREET
DSM	2	107/11				SAMORA AVENUE/MIRAMBO STREET
DSM	3	322/32				SAMORA AVENUE/ MKWEPU STREET
DSM	4	230/59				SAMORA AVENUE
DSM	5	6/186022				SAMORA AVENUE/MOROGORO ROAD
DSM	6	124				SAMORA AVENUE/ALGERIA STTREET
DSM	7	265/122				SAMORA AVENUE
DSM	8	123				SAMORA AVENUE
DSM	9	454/160				NKURUMAH
DSM	10	139				INDIA STREET/AGGREY STREET
DSM	11	68/98				MOSQUE STREET
DSM	12	105/27				AZIKIWE STREET
DSM	13	40/48				UPANGA ROAD/OHIO STREET
DSM	14	2356/47				OHIO STREET
DSM	15	69				HAILE SELASSIE ROAD
DSM	16	2817/12				JAMHURI ST./AZIKIWE STREET
DSM	17	32/186045				SEA VIEW
DSM	18	48/186017				BRIDGE STREET/SAMORA AVENUE
DSM	19	49/186017				SAMORA AVENUE
DSM	20	27/186017				BRIDGE STREET/WINDSOR STREET
DSM	21	14/186006				UPANGA ROAD/KISUTU STREET
DSM	22	145/47				UPANGA ROAD
DSM	23	108/11				MIRAMBO STREET
DSM	24	154/103				SAMORA AVENUE
DSM	25	1524/101				INDIA STREET/MOROGORO ROAD
DSM	26	62/129				NKURUMAH STREET
CANNOT BE TRACKED						
DSM	27	186021/6				SAMORA AVENUE/RAILWAY STREET
DSM	28	68				HAILE SELASSIE ROAD
TANGA	29	10 KB.2				KING STREET/CUSTOM ROAD/HOSPITAL ROAD
TANGA	30	54 KB.2				USAMBARA STREET/ARAB STREET
TANGA	31	66 KB.XVI				RAS KAZONE
TANGA	32	60				RAS KAZONE
TANGA	33	89A				RAS KAZONE
TANGA	34	70 KB.XVI				RAS KAZONE
TANGA	35	72				RAS KAZONE
DSM		19/186024				CITY DRIVE
MUAHI		7				BOMA ROAD
TANGA		19/130528				RASKAZONE
TANGA		4/130527				RASKAZONE
TANGA		2/130506/2				SAMORA AVENUE/CUSTOM ROAD
TANGA		10/130513				USAMBARA STREET/ARAB STREET
DSM		48-49/136017				BRIDGE STREET/SAMORA AVENUE
DSM		27/186017				BRIDGE STREET/INDIRA GANDHI STREET
DSM		14/186006				GUANGA ROAD/KISUTU STREET
DSM		7/186055				UPANGA ROAD
DSM		79/186016				SAMORA AVENUE
DSM		4/186027				MIRAMBO STREET

NATIONALISED PROPERTIES

TITLE DEED NO	SQ. FT.	DATA AQUIRED	COMMENTS	DATE OF SURRENDER
186024/15		23/04/71	EXPORTERS TRADING/AL-SHAAF BARGAIN CENTRE	22/05/71
186027/1		25/06/71	DEMOLISHED (CONTRUCTION ON THE WAY)	23/07/71
186024/4		23/04/71	METRONEX/VAIL SPRING/TAHFIF/SHIVACOM	22/05/71
9725		23/04/71	RENDEZVOUS REST.&TZ MEAT(NOWMONEYLINK BUREAU DE CHANGE)	DO
186022/6		23/04/71	NHC FLAT	DO
1860/1		23/04/71	LUKU SHOP-CURRENTLY UNDER RENOVATION	DO
186022/3		23/04/71	NHC	DO
186022/2		23/04/71	NHC-SHOPS	DO
6510		13/08/71	PETTY SHOPS	7/9/1971
2770		23/04/71	PRISON SHOP (DUKA LA MAGEREZA)	22/05/71
7024		14/12/71	MANEK TRADING	DO
7753		25/07/71	OFFICES	23/07/71
7752		25/06/71	NEW CONSTRUCTION (OWNER: ACTIS COMPANY)/AKIBA COMM.BANK	DO
186055/20		25/06/71	OFFICES	DO
186035/23		21/05/71	RESIDENCE	DO
186007		14/12/71		31/01/72
7116		29/05/71	RESIDENCE	25/06/71
186017/48		23/04/71		22/05/71
186017/49				DO
7083		27/04/71		DO
7124		27/04/71		DO
7750		21/05/71	RESIDENCE	16/06/71
6819		21/05/71	OFFICE	DO
6828		23/04/71		22/05/71
2730		23/04/71	DEMOLISHED (NEW CONSTRUCTION ON THE WAY)	7/9/1971
		13/08/71	SHOPS	CERTIFICAT OF TITLE
186021/6		23/04/71	SHOPS	22/05/71
186035/14		21/05/71	RESIDENCE HOUSE	16/06/71
130506/2		23/04/71	TPA DISPENSARY	22/05/71
130513/10		23/04/71	RESIDENCE & WHOLESALE TRADE(2STOREYS)/NHC	DO
130528/19		23/04/71	RESIDENCE-HAKIM MANZIL	DO
130527/4		23/04/71	RESIDENCE HOUSE	DO
130527/48		23/04/71	RESIDENCE HOUSE	DO
130528/10		23/04/71	UNDER NATIONAL HOUSING CORP.(NHC)	DO
130527/47		23/04/71	UNDER NATIONAL HOUSING CORP.(NHC)	DO
186024/19		THE BOARD DECIDED ON 15/12/71 TO RESTORE THIS PROPERTY ON OUR APPEAL NO. AT/10		23/04/71
056021/28		THE BOARD DECIDED ON 23/09/72 TO RESTORE THIS PROPERTY TO US ON OUR APPEAL NO.AT/63		23/04/71
130523/19		23/04/71	HOUSE	
130527		23/04/71	HOUSE	
130506/2		23/04/71	GODOWN, SHOP, OFFICE, GODOWN	
130513/10		23/04/71	OFFICE	
186017/48, 186017/49		23/04/71	WHOLE BLDG. - HERITAGE MOTEL ROUNDABOUT	
7083		27/04/71	RESTAURANT GODOWN - HERITAGE MOTEL ROUNDABOUT	
7124		27/04/71	OFFICE/YARD GODOWN	
7750		21/05/71	TRANSAFRICA CONSORTIUS	
6828		23/04/71	OFFICE	
6819		21/05/71	FLAT	

TOWN	FILE NO	PLOT NO	C.E.P. LOT NO	NEW PLOT NO	BLOCK NO	STREET
DSM		53/186016				MOROGORO ROAD/INDIA STREET
DSM		6/186021				SAMORA AVENUE/RAILWAY STREET
DSM		14/186035				HAILE SELASSIE ROAD
DSM		15/186024				MKWEPU STREET
DSM		4/186024/4				SAMORA AVENUE/MKWEPU STREET
DSM		84/186016				SAMORA AVENUE
DSM		6/186022				SAMORA AVENUE/MOROGORO ROAD
DSM		3/186022				SAMORA AVENUE
DSM		2/186022				SAMORA AVENUE
DSM		1/186022				SAMORA AVENUE/ALGERIA STREET
DSM		10/186015				INDIA STREET/AGGREY STREET
DSM		14/186016				MOSQUE STREET
DSM		23/186035				HAILE SELASSIE ROAD
DSM	1	15			186024	MKWEPU STREET
DSM	2	4			186024	MKWEPU STREET/SAMORA AVENUE
DSM	3	84			186016	SAMORA AVENUE
DSM	4	6			186022	SAMORA AVENUE/MOROGORO ROAD
DSM	5	3			186022	SAMORA AVENUE
DSM	6	2			186022	SAMORA AVENUE
DSM	7	1			186022	SAMORA AVENUE/ ALGERIA STREET
DSM	8	10			186015	INDIA STREET/AGGREY STREET
DSM	9	14			186016	MOSQUE STREET
TANGA	10	54-KB.II				USAMBARA STREET/ARAB STREET
TANGA	11	66-KB.XVI				RAS KAZONE
TANGA	12	10-KB.II				KING STREET/CUSTOM HOUSE ROAD/HOSPITAL ROAD
TANGA	13	60				RAS KAZONE
TANGA	14	89				RAS KAZONE
TANGA	15	70-KB. XVI				RAS KAZONE
TANGA	16	72 KB XVI				RAS KAZONE
DSM	17	79			186016	SAMORA AVENUE
DSM	18	48			186017	BRIDGE STREET/SAMORA AVENUE
DSM	19	49			186017	SAMORA AVENUE
DSM	20	27			186017	BRIDGE STREET/WINDSOR STREET
DSM	21	14			186006	UPANGA ROAD/KISUTU STREET
DSM	22	6			186021	RAILWAY STREET/SAMORA AVENUE
TANGA		19/180528				RASKAZONE
TANGA		4/130527				RASKAZONE
TANGA		2/130506				SAMORA AVENUE/CUSTOM ROAD
TANGA		10/130513		54 KB II		USAMBARA STREET/ARAB STREET
DSM		48-49/186017				BRIDGE STREET/SAMORA AVENUE
DSM		27/186017				BRIDGE STREET/INDIRA GANDHI STREET
DSM		14/186006				UPANGA ROAD/KISUTU STREET
DSM		7/186055				UPANGA ROAD
DSM		79/186016				SAMORA AVENUE
DSM		4/186027				MIRAMBO STREET
DSM		53/186016				MOROGORO ROAD/INDIA STREET
DSM		6/186021				SAMORA AVENUE/RAILWAY STREET
DSM		14/186035				HAILE SELASSIE ROAD

NATIONALISED PROPERTIES

TITLE DEED NO	SQ. FT.	DATA AQUIRED	COMMENTS	DATE OF SURRENDER
186016/53		23/04/71	SHOP, FLAT	
186021/6		23/04/71	RESTAURANT, OFFICE, FLAT, BUNGALOW	
186035/14		21/05/71	HOUSE	
186024/15		23/04/71	WHOLE BUILDING	
186024/4		23/04/71	SHOP, STORE, FLAT	
9725		23/04/71	GROUND FLOOR SHOP, FLAT	
186022/6		27/04/71	SHOP, FLAT, GODOWNS	
186022/3		23/04/71	SHOP, GODOWNS. FLAT	
186022/2		23/04/71	GROUND FLOOR PREMISES, FIRST FLOOR PREMISES, REAR GODOWN	
186022/1		23/04/1971	OFFICE, REAR GODOWN, OFFICE, FLAT	
186015/10		23/04/71	SHOP, FLAT	
7024		7/5/1971	SHOPS, FLAT	
186035/23		21/05/71	FLAT	
186024/15				
186024/4			METROLEX/VAYLESPRING/SHIVACOM	
9725			RENDEZVOUS REST.&TZ MEAT(NOWMONEYLINK BUREAU DE CHANGE)	
186022/6			FLAT,SHOPS	
186022/3			FLAT-SHOPS,OFFICES	
186022/2			OFFICES	
186022/1			LUKU SHOP-CURRENTLY UNDER RENOVATION	
2770			PRISON SHOP	
7024			MANEK TRADING	
130513/10			RESIDENCE-UPSTAIRS,WHOLESALE-DOWNSTAIRS	
130506/2			RESIDENCE HOUSE	
130506/2			TANZANIA PORT AUTHORITY DISPENSARY/NHC	
130527/4			PRIVATE OWNED RESIDENCE	
130527/48			RESIDENCE HOUSE-PRIVATE OWNED	
130528/10			RESIDENCE HOUSE-PRIVATE OWNED	
135027/47			UNDER NATIONAL HOUSING CORP.(NHC)	
6828			OFFICE	
186017/48				
186017/49				
7083				
7124				
186021/6			SHOPS	
130528/19		23/04/71	RESIDENCE HOUSE	
130527/4		23/04/71	RESIDENCE HOUSE	
130506/2		23/04/71	TANZANIA PORT AUTHORITY DISPENSARY	
130513/10		23/04/71	RESIDENCE & WHOLESALE TRADE	
186017/48 186017/49		23/04/71	WHOLE BUILDING	
7083		27/04/71	RESTAURANT, GODOWN	
7124		27/04/71	OFFICE, YARD, GODOWN	
7750		21/05/71	TRANSAFRICA CONSORTIUM	
6828		23/04/71	OFFICE	
6819		21/05/71	FLAT	
186016/53		23/04/71	SHOP	
186021/6		23/04/71	RESTAURANT, OFFICE, FLAT, BUNGALOW	
186035/14		21/05/71	HOUSE	

Notes

1]   The title 'Merchant Princes of Africa' appeared in the *Caltex Star* publication Tanganyika Merchant Princes, *Caltex Star*, volume (3) 9, 1952, pp. 4-7.

2]   W.G. Clarence-Smith, "Indian and Arab Entrepreneurs in Eastern Africa, 1800-1914." In H. Bonin, M. Cahen (eds.) *Négoce blanc en Afrique Noire; l'évolution du commerce à longue distance en Afrique Noire, du 18e au 20e siècle*, pp. 335-349. Paris: Société Française d'Histoire d'Outremer.

3]   The connection between Buddhayboy Noormuhammed and Jairam Sewji is via Anverali Hassanali Noorani, who was the great-grandson of Jivanjee. He was born in 1901. Interview published in Cynthia Salvadori, *They came in Dhows*, Nairobi 1996, pp. 100-101. Information related to Jairam Sewji can be found in the Colonial Office (hereafter CO), Memo by Sir Bartle Frere, Correspondence 1856, p. 10. For success and failure in Indian businesses in Zanzibar see, G. Oonk, 'South Asians in East Africa (1880-1920) with a Particular Focus on Zanzibar. Towards a historical explanation of economic success of a middlemen minority'. *Journal of African and Asian Studies*, 2006 (1) pp. 57-89.

4]   See the notable works of M.N. Pearson, *Port Cities and Intruders* for this early period. *The Swahili Coast, India, Portugal in the Early Modern Area*, Baltimore and London 1998. K.N. Chaudhury, *Trade and Civilization in the Indian Ocean. An Economic History from the Rise of Islam to 1750*, Cambridge 1985 and by the same author, *Asia Before Europe. Economy and Civilization of the Indian Ocean from the Rise of Islam to 1750*, Cambridge 1990.

5]   Richard F. Burton, *Zanzibar City, Island and Coast*, (1872) reprint 2003 University Press of the Pacific, p. 366. At around the same time we find in Kirk's survey of Zanzibar & Dominions that in 1870 there were 250 Bohras in Zanzibar.

6]   See for differences between the settlement of Muslim and Hindu families in East Africa, G. Oonk, 'The Changing Culture of the Hindu Lohana Community in East Africa', *Contemporary Asian Studies*, 13 (1) 2004, pp. 7-23.

7]   Christie, James, *Cholera Epidemics in East Africa. An account of the several diffusions of the disease in that country from 1821 till 1872, with an outline of the geography, ethnology, and trade connections of the regions through which the epidemics passed*, Macmillan London 1876.

8]   Memo by Sir Bartle Frere, Correspondence p.101, Honey, *A History of Indian Merchants*, Unpublished PH-D thesis, Dar es Salaam University 1982 p. 63.

9]   Zanzibar Archives, Serial E. 28, outward letter No 3. of 1860 quoted in Mangat, *History of Asians*, p. 7.

10]   In an undated typed written document by Fazlebas Esmailjee Jivanjee it is said that he might have drowned during one of his trips from India to Zanzibar. Family Archive.

11]   The most comprehensive history of the 19th century Karimjee Jivanjee family, may be found in: Somerset Playne, *East Africa (British)*, 1909, pp. 420-423.

12]   In fact, Esmailjee Jivanjee assisted Sir John Kirk, the British Consul in Zanzibar to stop the slave trade. Somerset Playne, *East Africa (British). Its History, People, Commerce, Industries, and Resources*, published by The Foreign and Colonial Compiling and Publishing Company, 1909, p. 420.

13]   G. Oonk, 'South Asians in East Africa (1880 - 1920)', *Journal of African and Asian Studies*, 2006 (1) pp. 57-89.

14]   Somerset Playne, *East Africa (British)*, 1909, pp. 420-423; This was later partly re-published in the *Samarch* (1929) and the *Caltex Star* publication Tanganyika Merchants Princes, *Caltex Star*, volume (3) 9, 1952, pp. 4-7.

15]   Some of Abdulla's children stayed in the Hrumzi house when he went to Tanga to open up the estates after the First World War.

16]   Interview Fizza Hakim Karimjee, 04-07-2008.

17]   Somerset Playne, *East Africa (British)*, 1909, pp. 420-423.

18]   Somerset Playne, *East Africa (British)*, 1909, pp. 420-423.

19]   Her autobiography is E. Ruete, *Memoirs of an Arabian Princess from Zanzibar*, Gallery Publications Zanzibar 1998 [1886].

NOTES

20] R.F. Burton, *Zanzibar: City Island and Coast*, London Longman 1872, vol I 87.

21] Rau, Uwe and Mwalim A. Mwalim, *Doors of Zanzibar*, HSP publications London/Zanzibar 1998, p. 48.

22] See chapter 6 for more details on Sir Yusufali's political ambitions.

23] Passport and letter available in the KJ family archive.

24] Various newspaper cuttings. *Daily News* 03-07-1961; *Tanganyika Herald* 17-04-1969.

25] Robert G. Gregory, *India and East Africa. A History of Race Relations within the British Empire*, Clarendonpress 1971, p. 380.

26] *The Tanga Post and East Coast Advertiser*, 11 June 1921, p. 3.

27] *Samarch Silver Jubilee* number 1929, p. 47.

28] This was probably due to the fact that Indian businesses preferred to maintain the confidentiality of their businesses within their community. We lost our gift of expression. Loss of the mother tongue among Indians in East Africa, 1880 - 2000, in *Global Indian Diasporas. Exploring Trajectories of Migration and Theory*. G. Oonk (ed) Amsterdam University Press 2007, pp. 31-67. Here I argue that this followed some legal disputes between Indian traders and German officers who were unable to read account books, which were often written in Gujarati.

29] *Samarch Silver Jubilee* number 1929, p. 47.

30] Tanganyika Merchants Princes, *Caltex Star*, volume (3) 9, 1952, p. 5.

31] ibid

32] ibid

33] Hitchcock, Sir Eldred, *The Sisal Industry of Tanganyika*, Reprinted from the Tanganyika Trade Bulletin, 1955, p. 8.

34] Anver Karimjee, in Nicholas Westcott, 'The East African Sisal Industry, 1929-1949: The Marketing of a Colonial Commodity during Depression and War, *The Journal of African History*, 25 (4) 1984, p. 447.

35] G.W. Lock, *Sisal: 25 years of Sisal Research*, London 1962;

Parpart, L., and Rostgaard, M., *The Practical Imperialist. Letters from a Danish Planter in East Africa, 1888-1906*, Brill Leiden, Boston, 2007; Westcott, Nicholas, 'The East African Sisal Industry, 1929-1949: The Marketing of a Colonial Commodity during Depression and War, *The Journal of African History*, 25 (4) 1984, pp. 445-461.

36] Correspondence between Abdulla M.A. Karimjee and the Governor of Tanganyika Territory, family archive.

37] Narrated by Amir Karimjee. Karimjee Jivanjee family archive.

38] The Italian filmmaker Gualtiero Jacopetti and his crew shot (from a plane and a helicopter) footage of the operations as they took place, during the filming of his documentary Africa Addio, which premiered in 1966 and represents the only existing documentary of the mass murder and genocide.

39] See for the various impressions on the 'numbers' issue Oonk (2004); Gregory (1971) and others.

40] At different times younger family members joined him at KJ Estates - Hafiz Khandwalla (Yusufali's grandson) at the start of this period, and towards the end, Anver's son Saleem.

41] An offered price of around USD 3,000,000 is still circulating in the family. In fact the directors of the company already had an agreement with the Chandaria's which was subject to approval by the shareholders. This approval was not received. Therefore the business remained within the Karimjee Jivanjee family.

42] Karimjee Agriculture, Managing Director's Report 1997.

43] Karimjee Agriculture, Managing Director's Report 1997.

44] I am highly indebted to Salvadori, Cynthia for this. *Through Open Doors. A view of Asian Cultures in Kenya*, Nairobi 1989 (1983) 2nd edition, pp. 254-269. The core of the material on religion is taken from this excellent book. I only added specific 'Karimjee particulars'.

45] Salvadori, Cynthia. *Through Open Doors. A view of Asian*

Cultures in Kenya, Nairobi 1989 (1983) 2nd edition, pp. 254-269. See also Oonk, Gijsbert, *The Changing Culture of the Hindu Lohana Community in East Africa, Contemporary Asian Studies*, 13 (1) 2004, pp. 7-23.

46] Gregory Robert G., *The Rise and Fall of Philanthropy in East Africa. The Asian Contribution*, Transaction Publishers, London, 1992, pp. 1-11 and 21.

47] Salvadori, Cynthia. *Through Open Doors. A view of Asian Cultures in Kenya*, Nairobi 1989 (1983) 2nd edition, p. 262.

49] We may assume that their political presence was earlier, but we do not have records to support this assumption.

50] *India*, 17 September 1909.

51] Yusufali Esmailjee Jivanjee, *Memorandum on the Report of the Commission on Agriculture*, 1923. Poona 1924.

52] *The Tanganyika Herald*, 15 December 1934, p. 12.

53] *The Tanganyika Herald*, ibid 13.

54] K.P.S. Menon, *Report on the Marketing Legislation in Tanganyika, Uganda and Kenya*, Government of India Press 1934. Robert G. Gregory, *India and East Africa. A History of Race Relations within the British Empire*, 1890-1939, Oxford 1971, pp. 458-476.

55] *The Tanganyika Herald*, 17 July 1937, p. 10.

56] Pandit, Shanti (ed)., Asians in E. and Cen. Africa (Nairobi, Panco 1963, 67. Private conversation of Martha Honey 20 March 1973 with Yusufali Karimjee in Dar es Salaam.

57] *Tanganyika Opinion*, 9 May 1930.

58] Tanganyika Merchants Princes, *Caltex Star*, volume (3) 9, 1952, pp. 4-7.

59] I have counted an inflation rate of 7 per cent per annum. This is a rather conservative figure for East Africa.

60] *Tanganyika Standard*, April 18 1955.

61] Caltex: *Caltex Star* publication Tanganyika Merchants Princes, *Caltex Star*, volume (3) 9, 1952, pp. 4-7.

62] Mwangara 10 August 1960.

63] Please note that I have not included the numerous positions these people held in Rotary clubs, charitable organisations of others and interim jobs for the government, the World Health Organisation, etc.

64] Somerset Playne, *East Africa (British). Its History, People, Commerce, Industries, and Resources*, published by The Foreign and Colonial Compiling and Publishing Company, 1909, p. 420.